CAROLINE SAUNDERS

HOW TO KNOW THE GOSPEL
AND LIVE IT

ISBN: 978-1-0877-6306-4
Item: 005837471

Dewey decimal classification: 248.82
Subject heading: GIRLS / SALVATION / CHRISTIAN LIFE

Unless otherwise noted, all Scripture quotations are taken from the Christian Standard Bible®, Copyright © 2017 by Holman Bible Publishers. Used by permission. Christian Standard Bible® and CSB® are federally registered trademarks of Holman Bible Publishers. Scripture quotations marked (ESV) are from the ESV® Bible (The Holy Bible, English Standard Version®), copyright © 2001 by Crossway, a publishing ministry of Good News Publishers. Used by permission. All rights reserved.

To order additional copies of this resource, write Lifeway Resources Customer Service; 200 Powell Place, Suite 100, Brentwood, TN 37027; Fax order to 615.251.5933; call toll-free 800.458.2772; email orderentry@lifeway.com; or order online at lifeway.com.

Printed in the United States of America.

Lifeway Girls
Lifeway Resources
200 Powell Place, Suite 100
Brentwood, TN 37027

Editorial Team,
Lifeway Girls
Bible Studies

Ben Trueblood
Director,
Lifeway Students

John Paul Basham
Manager

Karen Daniel
Team Leader

Amanda Mejias
Content Editor

Morgan Hawk
Production Editor

Shiloh Stufflebeam
Graphic Designer

table of contents

about the author

Caroline Saunders is a writer, pastor's wife, and mother of three who believes in taking Jesus seriously and being un-serious about nearly everything else. She is passionate about helping women and girls know, love, and enjoy God and His Word! Her Lifeway Girls study *Better Than Life: How to Study the Bible and Like It* is designed to help girls to know, love, and enjoy the Lord by equipping them to study the Bible—and her new study *Good News: How to Know the Gospel and Live It* is designed to help girls react to the world with the marvelously good news of the gospel. Caroline loves to serve in her home, at her church, and through the parachurch women's ministry Story & Soul, and she is always accidentally cooking items that should not be cooked. (Spoons, usually. Pray for her.) Find her writing, resources, and ridiculousness at writercaroline.com and on Instagram @writercaroline.

Note from the Author

Dear sisters,

A few years ago, someone confronted me with a list of things that person believed I'd done wrong. A meticulous record of sins. About half of what this person said was completely untrue, a fourth of it only partially true, but that fourth that was true? Well, it was a gut punch. Deeply horrified, I felt sick to my stomach for a full day. As every cell seemed to twist in concern, I attempted to go about my regular life, but every few minutes, I had to stop and cry.

It is not easy to be confronted with your sins. In fact, I physically found it hard to breathe under the shame of it. To cope, I talked with my husband, my parents, a good friend—all people who know me and know Jesus. They were totally on my side, saying things like, "I can't believe that person said that!" and "It says way more about that person than it says about you," but these conversations only offered momentary reprieve. Honestly, I suspected this person saw something my loved ones couldn't—that there was a fraction of truth buried within those harsh words. I had caught a glimpse of myself, and it was devastating. The experience was like an emotional hurricane: I was mad at the confronter whose words made me feel betrayed and exposed, but I was also ashamed of myself and wanted to crawl into a hole. All of it felt like too much to bear.

Forty-eight hours later, as I was driving in my car, still wrestling with my sin, shame, and anger, the Holy Spirit flicked a gospel light switch in my head. It was as if Jesus himself whispered into my ear, "Caroline, my blood covers this list. You are free. You are safe."

In that moment, a different kind of tears came, and I started to laugh with relief and joy! Suddenly, I realized the solution wasn't to blame the person who confronted me, to point out the untruths, to rationalize my behavior, or to have dramatic conversations with anyone who would share in my anger and blame. The solution was the gospel.

I began to follow Jesus when I was eight years old, and the gospel was familiar to me. I knew it in a responsible, dutiful way, like a grocery list: eggs, milk, flour, sugar, butter. Jesus had forgiven my sins and saved me from eternal judgment in hell. But how had I missed that the gospel is good news not just for my eternal life, but for my everyday life? That day in the car was one of the first times I understood that the gospel is really good news—like the kind of good news that makes you jump up and down and throw confetti.

Slowly, I began to grasp the gospel beyond grocery list knowledge. The eggs, milk, flour, sugar, butter thing wasn't wrong—it just wasn't the full picture. I began to understand it the way I understand that eggs, milk, flour, and sugar can be combined in just such a way and baked at a certain temperature for a certain length of time, and the scent will fill the kitchen. How they become something new, and that thing can be placed on a platter, slathered with icing, and topped with sprinkles and a specific number of candles. How those candles can be illuminated and accompanied with a song, sung by people who love me, who want to bear witness to a milestone in my life.

In this study, I'll teach you the grocery list stuff, but I also want to point you to the birthday cake stuff. Yes, the gospel is a list of biblical truths, but it's also delicious and beautiful. It's being loved and cherished and considered and counted. It's belonging and home and safety. It's being sung over and delighted in. It's the terrible list being truly covered—thank you, Jesus! It's good news for your eternity and your every day—including this day.

That moment in the car, the gospel's goodness was gloriously specific to me: God had wholly seen me—every sin exactly as bad as it actually is, listed out in perfect detail. But rather than cruelly expose me, God covered it with the blood of Jesus so that the sin and shame wouldn't crush me, so that He could be with me. I could cry about this. (I know! So much crying!) God is not like anyone else.

If you've never cracked open a Bible or set foot in a church in your life, the gospel is good news for you, right this very moment. And for church girls like me—well, we make this big mistake in which we assume the gospel is a thing that saves us and then can set aside. Trust me, it is good news for you, too, right this very moment.

Spiritually speaking, things may seem very gray-scale to you right now—all black and white and list-like and humdrum and orderly. But knowing the gospel in a deeper way has the power to make everything full color. Let's allow the gospel to color the way we look at the world, like a great pair of glasses.

Get ready—there's good news ahead.

Your sister,

how to use

Before you navigate the seven components of the gospel over our eight sessions together, I have three parts of this Bible study that I want to highlight:

GROUP TIME

My hope is that you won't attempt to do this study on your own. Invite your friends, mom, leader, or that girl who sits alone at the school lunch table to join you for this study of the gospel. The Group Time will be the intro for each week of personal study, so you want to always make sure you start here.

This section is full of questions and review to help your group go deep in discussion with one another. You will also want to watch the teaching videos (available for separate purchase) to help shape your view of each gospel element and hear how each offers really, really good news.

PERSONAL STUDY

Each session contains three days of Personal Study that you can complete anytime before your next Group Time. You will want to make sure you have a Bible and a pen ready, because there will be so many ways for you to interact and discover God's Word for yourself.

DISCOVERY

There's probably some part of your life right now where you'd really love some good news. At the end of each session, I'll invite you to practice wearing your gospel glasses by looking at your own life, considering where you're hungry for good news, and how the gospel offers it. The purpose of these pages is to help you take what you've learned from just pure head knowledge and ask God to transform it into real heart and life change. This will be so much fun and so purposeful, so don't skip it when you get to the end of each session!

The gospel is the good news story of **1** God rescuing a **2** sinful world by sending His Son Jesus to **3** live the perfect life no one could live, **4** die a punishing death sinners deserve, and **5** miraculously defeat death by coming back to life! Jesus returned to heaven but sent the **6** Holy Spirit to help everyone that would follow Him, and He promised to **7** return again to finally make everything wonderful forever.

SESSION 1

Group time

THIS STUDY IS ALL ABOUT GOOD NEWS!

What's some good news you got this week?

What's some bad news you got this week?

Is there any good news hidden inside the bad news?

INTRODUCTION

Here are three things to know about the gospel:

1. It means "good news."

2. The gospel is good news that grows, making more good news everywhere we look.[1]

3. This good news isn't snobby and complicated. It isn't just for cool kids or smart people or talented people. It is simple, and it is for everyone. It's for you!

Oh, and one more thing: The gospel starts with God. In fact, everything starts with God. But who is God?

When we want to know someone, one of the first things ask is, "What's your name?" So, let's start with God's name.

♥ You may know already that God has lots of names. Can you list a few names of God?

♥ Read Isaiah 9:6 and Isaiah 44:6 in your Bible. Write down every name of God that you see in these two verses.

♥ Though God has lots of names, He has one name that is His personal name. What is the name that your close friends and family call you?

WATCH

As you watch the Session 1 video with your group, fill in the blanks below.

The Hebrew word for God seen throughout Genesis is _____.

Elohim likes to use _____ to accomplish His good ideas, but he doesn't _____ that they do it alone. He promises to be _____ them.

In your Bible, anytime you see the word _____ written in all caps, this is an indication of the divine name:_____.

Here's a weird word to help you remember what God's name means:

L — _____

U — _____   C —_____

P — _____

S — _____

It's not just His _____—it's what He's _____.

EXAMINATION

As we learned today, God's personal name is Yahweh.[2] We can find it in our Bibles when we see the word "Lᴏʀᴅ" written in all caps. This name is constructed from the Hebrew phrase "I Am Who I Am." We could talk about what it means for hours, but for now, remember the four things we learned with this totally made-up word: **LUPS.**

1. **Limitless:** Yahweh has no limits of time, space, or knowledge. For all time, "I AM."

2. **Unchanging:** Yahweh doesn't change. No matter what, "I AM."

3. **Present:** Yahweh is present everywhere. Wherever we go, "I AM."

4. **Self-existent:** Yahweh isn't influenced or made to be who He is. He simply is "I AM."

♥ Read Exodus 33:11-23 below. This is just before Yahweh passes before Moses and proclaims His name. As you read, circle every mention of the divine name.

> [11] The Lᴏʀᴅ would speak with Moses face to face, just as a man speaks with his friend, then Moses would return to the camp. His assistant, the young man Joshua son of Nun, would not leave the inside of the tent. [12] Moses said to the Lᴏʀᴅ, "Look, you have told me, 'Lead this people up,' but you have not let me know whom you will send with me. You said, 'I know you by name, and you have also found favor with me.' [13] Now if I have indeed found favor with you, please teach me your ways, and I will know you, so that I may find favor with you. Now consider that this nation is your people." [14] And he replied, "My presence will go with you, and I will give you rest." [15] "If your presence does not go," Moses responded to him, "don't make us go up from here. [16] How will it be known that I and your people have found favor with you unless you go with us? I and your people will be distinguished by this from all the other people on the face of the earth." [17] The Lᴏʀᴅ answered Moses, "I will do this very thing you have asked, for you have found favor with me, and I know you by name." [18] Then Moses said, "Please, let me see your glory." [19] He said, "I will cause all my goodness to pass in front of you, and I will proclaim

*the name 'the L*ORD*' before you. I will be gracious to whom I will be gracious, and I will have compassion on whom I will have compassion."* [20] *But he added, "You cannot see my face, for humans cannot see me and live."* [21] *The L*ORD *said, "Here is a place near me. You are to stand on the rock,* [22] *and when my glory passes by, I will put you in the crevice of the rock and cover you with my hand until I have passed by.* [23] *Then I will take my hand away, and you will see my back, but my face will not be seen."*

♥ Verses 12 and 17 tell us Yahweh knows Moses by name. Underline this info in the passage. But Moses never said, "Hi! My name is Moses." Why do you think Yahweh knows Moses's name?

Knowing everything is Yahweh's thing. Of course He knows Moses's name! In your Bible, look up Psalm 139. This psalm is written by King David and starts with "Yahweh."

♥ List some of the things David says Yahweh knows about him. (Hint: Look at verses 1-4,16.):

♥ Skip back to look at the Exodus 33 passage again.

1. In verse 13, what does Moses ask Yahweh to do?

2. How does Yahweh respond (v. 14)?

3. In verse 18, what does Moses ask Yahweh to do?

Glory means greatness, splendor. It implies a heaviness.[3] Imagine lifting a soaking wet towel that's fallen into a pool. It feels weighty because it's saturated with water. The idea of glory is like that—something soaked with wonderfulness. In essence, Moses is saying, "Show me every ounce of how amazing you are! Show me everything wonderful about you!"

♥ In response to this request, God says He will do four things. Go back to the text and number each one. (Hint: See verse 19.)

This list shows us some of the things that make God absolutely soaked with wonderfulness!

♥ Look up Exodus 34:5-9. This is where Yahweh proclaims His name to Moses. List some of the things this tells you about Yahweh:

♥ In the teaching video, we added a C for *character* to the front of our weird word, making it "CLUPS." How does God's character enhance your understanding of the LUPS traits?

APPLICATION

There isn't enough paper in the world to list all of things that make Yahweh wonderful. The list becomes more wonderful when we realize that Yahweh brings all His wonderfulness near to people. Look how God responds to Moses in his moments of fear:

♥ Back in Exodus 3, when Moses first met God and God asked him to be his tool to rescue the people, God responded to Moses's fear like this: "I will certainly be _____ you" (v. 12).

♥ In Exodus 33, Moses is leading those he rescued, and he seems overwhelmed. God offers these words to Moses in verse 14: "My presence will go _____ you."

In both of these situations, Moses has two big questions on his heart:

1. He wants to know the same thing we asked at the beginning: "Who is God?"

2. He also wants to know: "Are You coming with me?"

These two questions are buried within the heart of every human. When they pop up in your heart, how might you answer them, especially now that you have learned more about Yahweh?

♥ Practice answering below, so you can reference this page when your heart begins to wonder:

1. Who is God?

2. Is He with me?

PRAY

Close in prayer, praising God for the good news of the gospel and asking Him to help you and your group to grasp it in a deeper way.

Good News for When You Want Control and for When Things Feel Out of Control

---

Sometimes I think a life remote control would be amazing. Wouldn't it be great to mute someone annoying, fast-forward a boring class, or rewind back to a fun weekend?

Even more: Wouldn't it be nice to be able to "change the channel" when something horrible happens? Or to pause and savor wonderful moments?

The desire for control makes sense—We long to be safe from the unexpected.

♥   What is something you are trying to control in your life?

♥   What is something that feels out of control right now?

♥   What is something you know you can't control, and it feels helpless?

Let's look for good news for the girl who wants control and the girl who feels like everything is out of control.

♥   Open your Bibles to Psalm 121.

We don't know who wrote this psalm, but it's called a "Song of Ascents," which means it was likely designed for God's people to sing or recite as they traveled to Jerusalem for one of the important feasts.[4] Along their journey, they were able to remember important truths about Yahweh.

♥   As you read, circle every reference to the divine name (Yahweh = LORD). Keep in mind what we learned about His name (CLUPS).

♥   Where does help come from (vv. 1-2)?

♥ Who is awake when God's people are still asleep (and are unable to control anything) (vv. 3-4)?

♥ Who protects God's people (vv. 5-8.)?

This passage may bring difficult questions to the Christian's mind: *What about those times when I was obviously unsafe? When my foot slipped? When I was harmed?*

♥ What other difficult questions come to mind? (By the way, it's okay to wrestle with such questions. They are not too big for Yahweh!)

When a dancer turns, she must fix her gaze on an unmoving spot in order to stay steady while she spins. This concept is just as true for the Christian. So, let me show you your "spot":

♥ Read Exodus 34:5-8 and make a list of every quality of Yahweh's. As you make your list, remember Yahweh's name is built around the phrase "I Am Who I Am." That means in the past, present, and future, Yahweh stays how He is.

Sister, do things feel as if they're swirling out of control? Hear this good news: *what is chaos to you is not chaos to Yahweh.*

He is Yahweh. Everything is within His control, and you can trust Him because He is good. He always has been in control and good, He always will be in control and good, and He is, this moment, in control and good.

♥ Insert whatever problem is bothering you:

_____ is within God's control.

Does this truth mean all the questions melt away? No, but it means when the world spins, we have something steady and unchanging to look to.

And that's good news.

PERSONAL STUDY 2

Good News for When Your Past Is Broken and Your Future Is Uncertain

Sometimes terrible things in our past and unknown things in our future make us feel overwhelmed and unseen, like a blade of grass caught up in the whirl of a tornado. Where is the good news for the girl with the broken past? For the girl with the uncertain future?

The good news is that there is a God who loves and leads her without being bound by time. Consider what we've learned about the name Yahweh. It's built on that Hebrew phrase, "I Am Who I Am," and means in the past, present, and future, God is. God exists in those places that escape your grasp in the present moment, and in those places, He is Who He always is!

♥ Read Psalm 139 in your Bible.

1. What name does David use in verse 1?

2. Read verses 7-10. Wherever David goes, where is Yahweh?

3. Is there anywhere David can go that Yahweh is not?

4. Read verses 13-16a. Who formed David's inward parts?

5. Who knitted him together in his mother's womb?

6. What was not hidden from God?

7. In other words, before David was born, what did Yahweh see and what was He doing?

8. Read verse 16b. Before David was born, what did Yahweh have written down?

9. Consider verses 13-16. Is there any "when" David can go that Yahweh is not?

There is no **where** and no **when** David can go that God is not. We call this omnipresence—Yahweh is present everywhere!

This song (*psalm* means song!) was written by David to God, but it was given to the choirmaster for all of God's people to use in worship. (Notice the tiny superscription at the top of the psalm.) This means you can sing this song to God, too. So let's apply God's Word to your specific situation.

♥ Who formed your inward parts?

♥ Who knit you together in your mother's womb?

♥ What was Yahweh seeing and doing before you were ever born?

♥ Before you were born, what did Yahweh have written down?

♥ Is there anywhere you can go that God is not?

Sometimes we believe in God's **omnipresence**, but we don't believe in God's goodness. This is especially tempting when we don't understand what God was doing in our past or what God is planning for our future.

♥ Read the verses below and circle anything that has to do with the word "good":

> He said, "I will cause all my goodness to pass in front of you,
> and I will proclaim the name 'the LORD' before you."
> Exodus 33:19

> We know that all things work together for the good of those who love God,
> who are called according to his purpose.
> ROMANS 8:28

♥ In the first verse, Exodus 33:19, what connection do you see between God's name and God's goodness?

♥ Rewrite the second verse, Romans 8:28, in your own words.

To put it simply: God is good, and God works with goodness. Though our stories can feel random or cruel, God never operates with randomness or cruelty. Rather, He carefully weaves our stories for ultimate, eternal good in ways only a limitless, good God can! We may not get it today, but one day we will.

♥ In Psalm 139, David was praising God, but that doesn't mean he understood what God was doing. Read verse 6 and write it below:

When you don't understand what God is doing, you can say that, too: "This wondrous knowledge is beyond me. It is lofty; I am unable to reach it." It's normal to feel small, confused, and limited—but you get to trust in a limitless good.

Finally, take another look at verse 17. These verses are words of praise David offers to the One who saw him in every past moment and who holds every future day in His hands.

♥ Write them down in the space below as a song of praise to Yahweh:

♥ What is the good news for the girl whose past or present overwhelms her?

Good News for When Nothing Makes Sense and Everything Is a Mess

Earlier this week, we read about when God told Moses about Himself by causing all of His goodness to pass in front of Moses and proclaiming His name.

❤ What are some things God told Moses about Himself (Ex. 34:5-7)?

❤ Do you remember Moses's response (Ex. 34:8)? Write it below.

There's an important takeaway here: Who God is, is always good news. And who God is, is who He always is. Are you tracking with me?

Here's another way to say it: God is the same good-news God when nothing makes sense and everything is a mess. We can see this really clearly in the book of Job.

Job is one of the oldest books in the Bible, and it describes the account of a man whose world has come crashing down.

❤ Read Job 1:13-19 and 2:7 and record some of the tragedies Job endured:

A large portion of the book features Job's friends, who are trying to encourage Him and make sense of everything, and honestly, they aren't much help. But finally, God Himself speaks, and everything changes.

Why? Because who God is, is always good news. It's news that breathes life into the deadliest of places and offers stability to the shakiest of places—even for someone like Job, who knows God really well already and whose world has totally fallen apart.

♥ In Job 38, God offers a series of rhetorical questions that show how gloriously big He is—and how gloriously small Job is in comparison. Read it in your own Bible and note a few verses that make you say, "Whoa."

God continues sharing about Himself for two more chapters, and Job is stunned.

♥ Read his response in Job 42:1-6:

> *¹ Then Job replied to the LORD:*
> *² I know that you can do anything*
> *and no plan of yours can be thwarted.*
> *³ You asked, "Who is this who conceals my counsel with ignorance?"*
> *Surely I spoke about things I did not understand,*
> *things too wondrous for me to know.*
> *⁴ You said, "Listen now, and I will speak.*
> *When I question you, you will inform me."*
> *⁵ I had heard reports about you,*
> *but now my eyes have seen you.*
> *⁶ Therefore, I reject my words and am sorry for them;*
> *I am dust and ashes.*

♥ Circle that phrase "too wondrous" in verse 3. Does it ring a bell? Read David's words in Psalm 139:6 below and circle the similar wording:

> *This wondrous knowledge is beyond me.*
> *It is lofty; I am unable to reach it.*

When Job, David, and Moses have a better glimpse of who God is, they are no longer overwhelmed by all they don't know. Instead, they worship the God who knows everything.

This is good news for us, too: God knows everything. We don't have to try to know everything or fight to hold life's remote control. Instead, we can remember who God is and we can willingly entrust ourselves to His care. In the unknown, we can trade anxiety for awe, responding like David and Job by saying, "God, I don't know what's going on! What you're doing is too wonderful for me" and by remembering who God is. He is Yahweh!

♥   What is something you wish you knew right now?

Now take that thing you don't know and view it again in light of who God is. He knows it. He knows you. He knows everything.

Discovery

GOOD NEWS FOR WHEN YOU _____

In our group session, we talked about Exodus 33 and how Moses has two big questions he is asking God:

    1. "Who are You?"

    2. "Are You coming with me?"

Right now, there is probably something happening in your life where your heart is crying out those two questions.

♥ Describe one area of your life where you are hungry for good news:

♥ Take a few minutes and flip through this week's study pages. (You might highlight your favorite parts so you can easily reference them later, when it's harder to remember who God is.)

Our main takeaway is that who God is, is always good news. But sometimes, we need to take a moment to pause and consider how who God is, is good news right here and right now. Based on all we've learned about Yahweh this week, what good news can you offer yourself for that place of struggle in your life?

Let's close with two gospel verses from Romans 10. Read them over carefully so you don't overlook their good news:

**For everyone who calls on the name
of the Lord will be saved.**
ROMANS 10:13

**If you confess with your mouth, "Jesus is Lord,"
and believe in your heart that God raised
him from the dead, you will be saved.**
ROMANS 10:9

We spend most of our time in this study talking about how the gospel is good news for our **everyday specifics.** But the gospel is also good news for our **eternal salvation.** Remember, anyone who calls upon the name of the Lord will be saved—from their sins, from death, to a family, forever. When we repent of our sins, we are no longer enemies but His beloved children. When we confess our sins and call upon the Lord to be our Savior, we are forgiven and fathered forever.

Is this something you sense the Holy Spirit is stirring in you to do? Do you desire to put yourself under God's loving leadership forever? If so, ask Him to save you! Then, tell someone who loves Jesus: "I am a Christian now!" so they can celebrate with you.

SESSION 2

Group time

THIS STUDY IS ALL ABOUT GOOD NEWS!

What's some good news you got this week?

What's some bad news you got this week?

Is there any good news hidden inside the bad news?

What good news can you remember from last week's group session and study days?

INTRODUCTION

Imagine that a crime has been committed against your family—perhaps someone has been kidnapped, or all of your money has been stolen and your family is struggling to survive. Then, imagine you are in court with your family, and the judge pronounces his verdict: "It's okay!"

Imagine the judge made this same pronouncement over and over again to lots of families, so that the crimes were seen as no big deal. Meanwhile, your family and many others are struggling to process and heal.

♥ Discuss with your group: Is this a good judge? Is this a kind judge? Why or why not?

With an example like this, it's easy to see that justice is a good thing because it is the force that upholds the law. It's also easy to see that the law is supposed to help communities thrive. However, it's tempting to resent God when He is just and when He gives His law.

♥ Have you ever resented God's law? Have you ever felt like God was unfair? (Feel free to be honest here. After all, Yahweh already knows everything.)

WATCH

As you watch the Session 2 video with your group, fill in the blanks below.

_____ is not okay. _____ is a big deal.

God created that _____ for Adam and Eve not to keep them from _____ but to help them _____.

Sin often doesn't seem like an _____, but it's actually our biggest_____.

_____ is an agent of destruction and death, and pretending like it's _____ just gives the _____ more room to kill and destroy.

_____ is too good to ignore the _____ that is within you.

_____ is not like the world—He will not ignore the _____ that has been committed _____ you.

The _____ is that Yahweh _____ and acknowledges your greatest_____. He will not _____ ignore it.

EXAMINATION

The Bible says sin—which is anything that breaks God's law—is a big deal. But what is the law?

♥ Read Matthew 22:37b-40 to see how Jesus summarized it.

God's law can be summed up in two ideas: Love God with all you have, and love your neighbor as yourself. So any time we don't do these things, we are sinning, and sin is a big deal. From this perspective, it's easy to see that every single person is a sinner.

💜 Read the verse below and circle the word that tells us how many people are sinners.

> *"For all have sinned and fall short of the glory of God."*
> ROMANS 3:23

Uh oh! All of us. So God's law is good, but we aren't good. If we really consider the law and hold it up to our lives, it's plain that we can't follow God's law all the time—or even most of the time. That's a problem.

Another problem we have is that sin doesn't often feel like a big deal.

💜 With your group, make a list below:

Sins that seem like a big deal:	Sins that don't seem like a big deal:

💜 Discuss with your group: How did you decide what went into each list? Did anyone in your group have differing opinions?

That's because human evaluation of sin will always get a bit wonky. We all have different opinions, and we have a tendency to view our sins less severely than we might view the sins of that rude kid at school.

Check out this quote from Martin Lloyd-Jones:

> You will never make yourself feel that you are a sinner, because there is a mechanism in you as a result of sin that will always be defending you against every accusation. We are all on very good terms with ourselves, and we can

always put up a good case for ourselves. Even if we try to make ourselves feel that we are sinners, we will never do it. There is only one way to know that we are sinners, and that is to have some dim, glimmering conception of God.[1]

Truly, we need to look to God and His Word for an accurate view of sin. After all, He's Yahweh! Who better to look to than the One who knows everything, sees everything, and invented everything—and somehow stays the same regardless of what's happening in the world?

So, in the midst of all this sin talk, let's remember who God is. He's Yahweh! And when He proclaimed His name before Moses and told Moses all about Himself, God mentioned some wonderful things, like how he's gracious and merciful, and abounding in steadfast love. But He also included the way He relates to sin.

He talks about it in two ways: (1) that He is always, always able to forgive any kind of sin, and (2) that He will always, always punish sin, in every generation.

♥ Read the passage below and number the two ways God describes His character as it relates to sin:

> [5] The LORD came down in a cloud, stood with him there, and proclaimed his name, "the LORD." [6] The LORD passed in front of him and proclaimed: The LORD—the LORD is a compassionate and gracious God, slow to anger and abounding in faithful love and truth, [7] maintaining faithful love to a thousand generations, forgiving iniquity, rebellion, and sin. But he will not leave the guilty unpunished, bringing the consequences of the fathers' iniquity on the children and grandchildren to the third and fourth generation. [8] Moses immediately knelt low on the ground and worshiped."
> EXODUS 34:5-8

Both of these things point to the fact that sin is a big deal. It's hard to fathom how both can be true, though!

♥ How can God always be able to forgive but also always punish sin? (This is a deep question, and it's okay if you can't come up with a perfect answer. We'll get to that.)

Have someone in your group recount what happened in Genesis 4 with Cain and Abel, and reflect on how God described sin in verse 7. Then, consider these questions together:

♥ What would it say about God if, after Cain killed Abel, God said, "It's okay!"?

♥ What did God say after Cain killed Abel? (Hint: Read Gen. 4:10.)

♥ Why is it actually kind of God to punish sin?

Fast forward to the end of Genesis 4. Verse 26 says, "At that time people began to call upon the name of the Lord."

♥ Why might the name of the Lord be good news to a world full of sin?

APPLICATION

♥ To convince you that God's Word says that sin is a big deal, look up the following verses and write down what they say about sin:

James 1:14-15	Romans 6:23

♥ Considering all of these verses and the passages we've studied today (Gen. 3–4), write down a summary of God's view on sin.

Sin is a big deal, but even as we consider the horrible reality of that, let's never forget Yahweh! Everything we learned last week about Yahweh is still wonderfully true. That is Yahweh's thing—being who He is always and no matter what.

♥ Read Exodus 34:5-8 again and read 1 John 1:7-9. Then consider the following questions:

1. The next time a sin doesn't feel like a big deal to you, what can you remember about God?

2. The next time a sin feels like a huge deal to you, what can you remember about God?

3. Why does admitting our sin feel dangerous? What do we know about God that can help us know that we are safe to confess sin to Him?

It's hard to think about sin and recognize how truly terrible it is, but ultimately, this reality check leaves us longing for a Savior. It makes us desperate for someone to show us compassion, for someone to give us grace, for someone to be slow to anger, for someone who could be overflowing with the kind of love that never gives up, even when we've done things that seem unforgivable.

Who do we know who's like that?

PRAY

Close in prayer, praising God for the good news of the gospel and asking Him to help you and your group to grasp it in a deeper way.

Good News for When You've Been Hurt and for When You've Hurt Someone Else

Last week, we talked a lot about how God has no limits. One angle of this is that God sees everything. Sometimes, that feels relieving: "Oh, God sees me!" Sometimes, that feels rattling: "Oh no, God sees me!"

Ultimately, being seen by God is good news for us, especially as it relates to sin. Think about these two scenarios:

1. When someone hurts us, we have the *relieving* reality that God sees how we've been hurt—and that He thinks it's a big deal. (Isn't it extra painful to be in pain but to feel as if no one sees you or thinks it's a big deal?) Furthermore, we can know God is compassionate to us, right where it hurts. Compassion is part of who He is! *What a relief.*

2. When we hurt someone else, we have the *rattling* reality that God sees the pain we have caused—and that He thinks it's a big deal. As this rattles us, we can remember that though our sin is a big deal, forgiving sin is part of who God is! We can always ask God to forgive us. *What a relief.*

God seeing us always results in relief, one way or another. Let's look at some biblical accounts that back this up:

A story of someone who was hurt by the sins of others:

In Genesis 16, we encounter the story of Hagar, a woman who had been hurt very deeply by abuse. As she fled those who were hurting her, she was all alone in the desert when she encountered Yahweh.

♥ Look up Genesis 16:13 and write down the name Hagar gave Him:

♥ Based on what you read in verse 13, how do you think Hagar felt being seen by God? Was Yahweh's limitless sight good news for her?

A story of someone who hurt others with their sin:

In 2 Samuel 11–12, we witness with horror how sin grows within the heart of King David and how it brings destruction and death. It seems to start with idleness that leads to lust then adultery then deception then murder. Whoa!

King David deeply hurt many people because he befriended sin, which of course, sought to devour him. David thought he was doing these things in secret, but God saw.

♥ Read 2 Samuel 12:1-15 and answer the questions below.

1. Nathan was a prophet, whose job was to tell people what God said. According to verse 1, who sent Nathan to confront David?

2. What evidence do you see in the text that God believes this sin is a big deal?

3. What evidence do you see in the text that God is able to forgive what seems unforgivable?

4. Even though there's so much pain in the story, how is Yahweh's limitless sight good news here?

♥ After this confrontation with Nathan, David famously wrote Psalm 51. Take a moment to read it and answer the questions below.

1. What evidence do you see in Psalm 51 that David knows his sin is a big deal?

2. What evidence do you see in Psalm 51 that David knows God's character? (Remember what we learned in Exodus 34:5-7.)

Being seen by God is always a relief, and that relief tends to impact the way we interact with others, making us quicker to ask for and offer forgiveness.

Can you imagine how wonderful the world would be if, whenever we hurt someone, we (1) recognized sin is a big deal, (2) wholeheartedly asked God for forgiveness, and in relief, (3) asked for forgiveness from anyone we hurt?

Wow! God's way is so, so good for the world.

♥ How can the good news that God sees you impact your relationship with Him and with others right now?

Abuse Disclaimer: These biblical texts and this topic may have prompted you to think about abuse you or another person has suffered. Today's study is meant to teach you about Yahweh's limitless sight (which is good news for anyone who has suffered abuse), but it is not intended to equip you to deal with an abuser. God is always, always grieved by abuse, and abuse needs to be brought to the light. However, you shouldn't do this alone. Please talk to a trusted adult and get all the help you need. This study is also not meant to be a thorough guide for helping you process the experience of abuse. It may have brought to mind some hard questions about your experience, about God, or about how you should respond. Please talk about these questions with a trusted adult or other mature believer. God's limitless sight means that He is near to the brokenhearted and desires to bring healing and hope to your suffering.

Good News for When You Want to Defend Your Sin and for When You Feel Defeated by Your Sin

When it comes to sin, we tend to have a few default responses:

We defend it. "No fair!" "It wasn't that bad!" "I didn't mean to!" "Stop judging me!"

We are defeated by it. "I'm the worst person in the world." "I hate myself."

We identify with it. "That's just who I am."

So it makes sense that we would long for the seemingly good news of "It's okay!" That response helps us dodge the discomfort of actually dealing with sin. But there is true good news we can turn to instead.

Let's study a really important verse, 2 Corinthians 5:21, using the Bible-reading recipe I taught in another study, *Better Than Life: How to Study the Bible and Like It.* The recipe is COIA: Context, Observation, Interpretation, Application.

C – CONTEXT *To best understand a passage or verse, we need to know about the words around the ones we're reading. We also need to know who wrote the words, to whom they wrote the words, what was going on in the world when it was written, and how they wrote the words.*

Paul, a great leader and missionary of the early church, wrote letters to the group of Jesus followers in Corinth. He wrote these letters mainly because he was upset by the sin they were battling, and he wanted to help them see clearly. He also warns the Jesus followers not to believe words that didn't come from God. He wants them to examine themselves: Are they truly following Jesus? Do they really understand the gospel? Has it changed their lives?

O – OBSERVATION *This means to pay attention to the words. We want to understand what they say.*

Now that we have some idea about the context, let's observe the verse.

♥ Read 2 Corinthians 5:21 several times in your Bible.

To better understand the verse, let's define a few words. Use what you've learned this week and an online dictionary to help form your definitions:

Sin:

Righteousness:

I – INTERPRETATION *This means to wrestle with the words. We want to understand what they mean.*

♥ Look up the following verses. How do they help you understand this verse?

1 Peter 2:24: _____

Galatians 3:13: _____

Isaiah 53:11: _____

♥ Now, consider 2 Corinthians 5:21 and answer the following questions:

1. Paul wanted the Corinthians to know who *defends* them against the enemy of sin. Who did it? How did He do it?

2. Paul wanted the Corinthians to know who *defeated* sin. Who did it? How did He do it?

3. Paul wanted the Corinthians to better understand their *identity*. Because of Jesus, which word best describes their true identity: sinful or righteous?

Tomorrow we'll complete the last part of the recipe (A – Application), but for now, do you have a better grasp of the good news of 2 Corinthians 5:21?

♥ To press it into your heart, rewrite the main idea of 2 Corinthians 5:21 in your own words:

Good News for When You're Crushing It and for When It All Comes Crashing Down

Let's finish up our study of 2 Corinthians 5:21 by doing the last part of the recipe, A for Application. (You may want to first look over your notes from yesterday.)

A – APPLICATION *This means to invite the words to change the way we think and live. We want to ask God to use the words to make us more like Him.*

Consider all you've learned about the truth in 2 Corinthians 5:21 and answer the following questions:

♥ Why do I not need to **defend** my sin? What is the good news for when I feel defensive of my sin?

♥ Why do I not need to feel **defeated** by my sin? What is the good news for when I feel like the worst person in the world?

♥ Why do I not need to make my sin my **identity**? If I follow Jesus, what is my true identity because of Jesus?

This week, we've established that sin is a big deal. (Are you tired of me saying that, yet?)

But as we emphasize sin and its impact on the world, I don't want you to fall into the trap of seeing sin and self as so big that God begins to seem small. It's human nature to feel on top of the world when we think we're behaving perfectly, and it's human nature to feel as if everything has come crashing down when we think we're not behaving perfectly. But here's the good news:

You're not all-powerful. **Yahweh is.**

You're not in control. **Yahweh is.**

You're not able to see and know everything. **Yahweh is.**

You're not perfect. **Yahweh is.**

♥ Look up Colossians 1:17. Who holds all things together?

♥ Look up Hebrews 1:3. Who sustains all things?

Sister, take heart. Your God is holding all things together. Close out your time today by answering the questions below considering the passages you've read this week. Feel free to use the references in parentheses if you need extra help.

When I am crushing it and feel like I'm perfect, the good news is (Rom. 3:23):
When I am crushed by the weight of my sin, the good news is (Rom. 3:24):
When I think I have no need for forgiveness, the good news is (1 John 1:8):
When I think I have done the unforgivable, the good news is (1 John 1:9):
When I feel like I'm holding it together, who truly holds all things together (Job 38:1-4; Col. 1:17)?
When I feel like I can't hold it together, who is holding all things together (Job 38:1-4; Col. 1:17)?

Discovery

GOOD NEWS FOR WHEN YOU _____

♥ Take a few minutes and flip through this week's study pages. Considering all we've talked about this week, what is really sticking with you?

From the terrible moment in Genesis 3, the whole world has been impacted by sin, bringing destruction and death. We want sin to not be a big deal, but the whole world, the pit in our stomach, and most importantly, God's Word testifies:

Sin is a big deal! It is a devouring enemy!

And yet, there is Yahweh. A God who is full of compassion and grace and never-giving-up love, who knows sin is a big deal and punishes it, but who has always been forgiving towards those who repent, who always will be forgiving towards those who repent, and who, this very moment, is forgiving toward those who repent.

Sister, take heart. Your God forgives, and no matter how big sin seems, He is holding all things together.

So yes, our main takeaway is that sin is a big deal, but because of who God is, it is ultimately good news for us to agree with Him that our sin is a big deal.

♥ Take a moment to pause and consider how that big idea intersects with your current struggles. Where are you struggling? Where are you hungry for good news?

♥ Based on all we've learned about Yahweh and sin this week, what good news can you offer yourself for that place of struggle in your life?

Let's close with two gospel verses. Read them over carefully so you don't overlook their good news:

He made the one who did not know sin to be sin for us,
so that in him we might become the righteousness of God.
2 CORINTHIANS 5:21

Christ redeemed us from the curse of the law by becoming
a curse for us, because it is written, Cursed is everyone
who is hung on a tree. The purpose was that the blessing
of Abraham would come to the Gentiles by Christ Jesus, so
that we could receive the promised Spirit through faith.
GALATIANS 3:13-14

We spend most of our time in this study talking about how the gospel is good news for our **everyday specifics.** But the gospel is also good news for our **eternal salvation.** Christ became sin and a curse so that we could be delivered from sin and its curse! We simply do not have to live under all of that. Instead, we get to believe in Jesus's work on the cross, agree with God about our sin, and invite Him to forgive us and make us His! When we repent and trust in Jesus, we are no longer His sin-soaked enemies but forgiven and fathered forever.

Is this something you sense the Holy Spirit is stirring in you to do? Do you desire to put yourself under God's loving leadership forever? If so, ask Him to save you! Then, tell someone who loves Jesus: "I am a Christian now!" so they can celebrate with you.

P.S. Some people feel the nudge to "get saved" a lot. But once you are God's child, you are His child forever! You don't have to keep joining the family. If you are confused about this, ask a trusted Christian leader to help you discern it. You may consider reading 1 John or John 10:27-29 together.

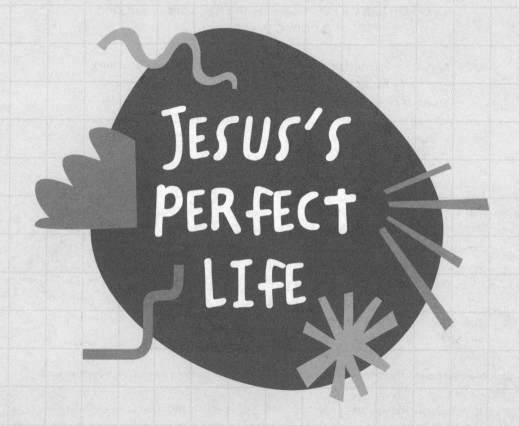

JESUS'S PERFECT LIFE

SESSION 3

Group time

THIS STUDY IS ALL ABOUT GOOD NEWS!

What's some good news you got this week?

What's some bad news you got this week?

Is there any good news hidden inside the bad news?

What good news can you remember from last week's group session and study days?

INTRODUCTION

♥ We've talked about who God is—who He really is. What do you remember about that?

♥ We've also talked about sin. What do you remember about that?

Now, we get to talk about Jesus! He is Yahweh's plan to rescue the sinful world. And this rescue unfolds in three important parts, all of which are good news for you: (1) Jesus's perfect life, (2) Jesus's punishing death, and (3) Jesus's miraculous new life. This week, we'll talk about Jesus's perfect life.

♥ *Perfect* is a word we have a complicated relationship with. What do you think about when you hear the word "perfect"?

When we say Jesus lived a perfect life, we are talking about His character. From the inside out, Jesus perfectly obeyed the law.

♥   What do you remember about the law? (Read Matt. 22:37b-40 if you need help.)

WATCH

As you watch the Session 3 video with your group, fill in the blanks below.

This baby was the _____ that Yahweh saves.

This baby was the _____ by which Yahweh would save.

This baby was Yahweh_____.

Jesus's perfect _____ is good news for you because of a beautiful _____truth called_____.

This is how imputation happens: We see that we are not _____ and that we need _____desperately to be our_____.

When Christ changes our_____, our _____changes our _____.

EXAMINATION

In Jesus's famous sermon, The Sermon on the Mount, His words likely rattled hearers because He seemed to take the law to a new, more impossible level. Let's go backwards through Matthew 5 to see some examples of this:

♥   Read Matthew 5:21-22,27-28. How do Jesus's words here seem to take the requirements of the law to a new level?

♥ Read Matthew 5:20. Despite the categories we place ourselves in, according to Jesus, how righteous do we need to be to enter the kingdom of heaven?

♥ Remember Romans 3:10 and 3:23 from last week? Look those verses up. Does anyone have what it takes to enter the kingdom of heaven?

♥ No one can fulfill the law! Well, actually, one person can and did. Read Matthew 5:17. Who fulfilled the law?

♥ Mark on the scale below where you consider yourself to be:

a spiritual
perfectionist

somewhere in
between

an "obvious"
sinner

Matthew 5 is convicting no matter how righteous we look on the outside. Jesus is clear that it's not just the appearance of following the law that matters—we have to be following it from the inside out.

♥ Look up Matthew 5:20 and 23:27-28.

In both of these verses, Jesus is talking about the scribes and the Pharisees, who are the spiritual perfectionists of Jesus's day.

♥ What does He say about their righteousness in 5:20?

♥ What does He say about their righteousness in 23:27-28?

These men have been trying really hard to be righteous, and they still don't meet the requirements of the law! In fact, the way they break the law seems to be extra offensive because it's dishonest—appearing one way on the outside, while being the exact opposite on the inside. They need to be changed from the inside out.

♥ What hope is there for any of us to become righteous? Or better yet— who is the hope for us to become righteous?

♥ In the teaching video, we learned a fancy theology word: imputation. Use 2 Corinthians 5:21 and an online dictionary to help you define it.

♥ If you have a giant, towering stack of sin you need to pay for (which is true for everyone!), imputation is really good news. In Christ, what is that giant stack of sin exchanged for?

♥ Since we've been talking about Matthew 5 backwards, rewind all the way to verse 6. Based on what you've learned about imputation, how does God satisfy those who are hungry and thirsty for righteousness?

APPLICATION

♥ Romans 10:13; Acts 2:21; and Joel 2:32 all say the same thing. What is it?

♥ Read Exodus 34:5-8. What does this passage teach us about the Lord through His name?

This is how imputation happens: We see that we are not righteous and that we need Christ desperately to be our righteousness. When we call upon the name of the Lord, we are saying, "Yahweh, I know You are compassionate and gracious and abounding in steadfast love, and that You can forgive the unforgivable! I know that's who You are! Be that for me!"

And then, He will. *Imputation!* Christ's righteousness is put in place of that towering stack of sin that would have crushed you. When Yahweh sees you, He sees the perfect account of His beloved Son.

This changes everything. When Christ changes our *status*, our status changes our *steps*. Our new status before God motivates us to use our energy to live in step with God's law. It motivates us to live in a way that honors Jesus's life and brings life to those around us.

♥ Read Matthew 5:13-16. What are the two metaphors Jesus uses to describe how those who are in Christ should live?

♥ If you are a Christ follower, where are areas in your life in which you have forgotten your status and have therefore not been living in step with His life-giving law? How might remembering your status transform your steps?

If you are not a Christ follower, you can call upon the name of the Lord! Will you consider talking with your group leader about this? God alone can change your status and provide rescue from death into life.

♥ Together with your group, complete this sentence: Jesus's perfect life is good news for me because _____

_____.

♥ How can you remind yourself of the good news of Jesus's perfect life the next time you're trying to be righteous on your own?

♥ How can you remind yourself of the good news of Jesus's perfect life the next time you're overwhelmed by the giant stack of sin in your life?

PRAY

Close in prayer, praising God for the good news of the gospel and asking Him to help you and your group to grasp it in a deeper way.

Good News for When You Think You're Strong and for When You Know You're Weak

In your group session, we talked about one fancy theology word: *imputation*. Can you remember what that means?

Today, we're going to investigate another fancy theology word—not because it's fancy, but because it's good news. It's good news for when you think you're strong and for when you know you're weak. The word is *incarnation*.

The word comes from the Latin word *incarnare*, which means "to make flesh."[1] Incarnation describes the part of the gospel when God Himself came to earth as a human. Jesus was fully God and fully man.

For some insight into the incarnation, look up John 1:1-14 in your Bible. As you read, you might consider circling the parts of the text that reveal Jesus's humanity (human-ness), and underlining the parts of the text that reveal Jesus's divinity (God-ness).

♥ Read John 1:1-14, then answer the questions below:

1. Who is "the Word"?

2. Is "the Word" God (v. 1)?

3. Record three other facts about "the Word."

4. Fill in the blanks: "The Word became _____ and dwelt among us" (v. 14).

In this passage, John is letting us know that Jesus isn't just Yahweh's message of salvation for the world (v. 1), Yahweh's means of salvation for the world (v. 12), and Yahweh's Son (v. 14)—He is Yahweh (v. 1) who came to earth as a human (v. 14). Is your brain a pretzel yet?

It's crazy news worth repeating: To rescue a sinful people, the limitless God of the universe came to earth as a limited human. Compare all humans need to survive (sleep, food, water, clothing, shelter, etc.) with what Yahweh needs (nothing!). The idea that Yahweh would lower Himself to become a human is pretty bonkers.

It's tempting to think the idea of incarnation doesn't have anything to do with our lives right now, but Jesus offers us good news in both His humanity (human-ness) and in His divinity (God-ness). Think about it:

The incarnation is really good news for when you think you're strong.

The God of the universe embraced human limitation, and you can, too. You cannot do it all, but you can trust the One who can.

♥ Where are you trying to be strong on your own?

♥ Here's a tough question: Are you pretending to be God by denying your human limitations? If so, how can you rest in your human limits and allow God to be the unlimited one?

♥ When you think you're strong, what good news can you tell yourself?

May Jesus's humanity free you to embrace your limits, and may His divinity humble you to trust Him to be your source of strength!

The incarnation is also really good news for when you know you're weak.

Rest, dear sister. The God of the universe knows what it's like to be weak. When your knees shake, when you're too tired to think straight, when your body is overcome by pain: Jesus knows what it is like.

In 2 Corinthians 12:9-10, Paul tells believers in a city called Corinth about a difficulty he was enduring—something that made him feel very weak and overwhelmed. Instead of removing this weakness, God offered something else.

Read these verses and keep an eye out for what God offered Paul.

> But he said to me, "My grace is sufficient for you, for my power is perfected in weakness." Therefore, I will most gladly boast all the more about my weaknesses, so that Christ's power may reside in me. So I take pleasure in weaknesses, insults, hardships, persecutions, and in difficulties, for the sake of Christ. For when I am weak, then I am strong.
>
> 2 CORINTHIANS 12:9-10

♥ What was Paul's new perspective on weakness?

♥ Where do you feel weak?

♥ When you know you're weak, what good news can you tell yourself?

May Jesus's humanity comfort you that you are not alone in your weakness, and may His divinity strengthen you!

Good News for When You're on Stage and for When You're Behind the Scenes

Jesus is probably the most famous person ever. Even non-religious people seem to have heard of Him. We have tons of information about certain events in His life, but there are also big chunks we don't know anything about.

💜 **Read John 21:25 out loud.**

The mystery stems even further. Before Jesus began His life of public ministry and miracles around the age of thirty, His life was pretty quiet. Regardless of whether He was "on stage" or "behind the scenes," Jesus lived perfectly—and this is good news for you.

Being "on stage" (literally or figuratively) can be fun and being "backstage" (literally or figuratively) can be a relief, but both are challenging.

💜 **Read the list below and circle any that make you say, "That's me":**

a. *Being on stage can give an inflated sense of importance. We might believe our feelings and problems matter more than others and deserve everyone's full attention.*

b. *Being on stage can make us feel exposed. We might feel everyone is looking at and analyzing us, yet no one truly knows us.*

c. *Being on stage can make us believe we have to perform to be valuable. We might worry we'll lose the approval of others if we don't meet their standards.*

d. *Being backstage can make us feel useless or unimportant. We might feel slumped over in sadness or full of angry resentment.*

e. *Being backstage can make us feel unsure about who we are. We might feel overwhelmed or tempted to prove ourselves.*

f. *Being backstage can make us feel overlooked—like no one knows we exist, cares about what we do, or sees the details of our lives.*

Jesus's perfect life is good news for all of these challenges. Wedged right between Jesus's "backstage" life and His "on stage" life is the story of His baptism, which was a public sign of His commitment to obey Yahweh.

♥ Read Matthew 3:13-17, and then answer the questions below.

1. According to verse 15, why was Jesus baptized?

2. Write down a few things you remember about righteousness:

3. Then, write down what God the Father spoke over God the Son in verse 17.

Have you ever received or wanted to receive a public declaration of affection like this? Our hearts long to know that we are fully loved, truly seen, and wholeheartedly delighted in!

For this reason, the reality of imputation is extra exciting when we consider it in light of Jesus's baptism. (Remember, imputation is the biblical concept that Jesus exchanges our sinfulness for His righteousness.) Because Jesus's baptism is connected with Jesus's righteousness (v. 15), God the Father's beautiful words over God the Son represent His posture toward all of His children!

Take a deep breath and pay close attention: If you follow Christ, it's as if God the Father looks at you and exclaims, "This is my beloved daughter, with whom I am well-pleased." Wow!

♥ Think about the "on stage" or the "backstage" challenge(s) that resonated with you. How are God the Father's words good news for that particular pain point?

Whether you're living in the spotlight or worry no one is watching, because of Jesus, you can bask in God the Father's delighted affection and let it satisfy that deep longing of your heart to be loved, seen, and delighted in.

♥ How might your life change if you really believed this part of the good news?

Good News for When You Want to Be Perfect and for When You Can't Do Anything Right

One afternoon in high school, my parents got on to me for my geometry grade. Geometry made zero sense to me (I also remember being distracted by at least one cute boy in my class), and I was lucky to be pulling off a C. My parents thought I could do better. They were right, and they were wise to challenge me, but I didn't handle the talk well. Instead, I flopped on my green and purple bed and cried my eyes out, saying, "I'm sorry I can't be perfect!" while visions of obtuse angles and the equation of a line haunted me.

In retrospect, it was dramatic. Also, the bedspread was a mistake. Also, the boy wasn't really that cute. Anyway.

I knew and loved Jesus at this point in my life, but frankly, I had no idea the gospel had any use beyond saving me from sin and hell. I didn't know that it could be good news for that day when I desperately wanted to be perfect but felt like an utter failure.

Maybe you can preach the good news to crying Caroline? Do 15-year-old me a favor, and look through what we've covered so far in this study to find verses and concepts that answer the questions below:

1. Who is the only One with all knowledge?

2. Who is the only One without limits?

3. Who is the only human who did everything perfectly?

4. When a person follows Jesus, what happens to their sin?

5. What do they receive instead?

6. Does a daughter's lack of self-control change God the Father's affection for her?

7. Does a daughter's lack of intelligence change God the Father's affection for her?

8. Does a daughter's limitations change God the Father's affection for her?

9. Does God the Father ever ask a daughter to earn His love and delight?

I want you to know that I'm smiling and a little teary thinking about how wonderful it would have been to have answered those questions that overwhelming day. Have you ever had a day like that?

♥ Tell me about it:

One of the wonderful things about the gospel is that it changes our hearts and minds—and then it changes our actions. Let's pretend 15-year-old Caroline has worked through her tears and is ready to take action. Help her understand how her *status* as daughter can impact her *steps*:

♥ As a beloved daughter, how can Caroline use geometry class as a way to honor the One who loves her?

♥ What's the good news for Caroline if she tries her best and still can't raise the grade?

♥ What's the good news for Caroline if she doesn't try her best?

♥ God the Father never asks His daughters to earn His approval. It's a free gift! And yet, why should Caroline still try her best? Read Colossians 3:23-24 and then answer.

Discovery Page

GOOD NEWS FOR WHEN YOU_____

♥ Take a few minutes and flip through this week's study pages. Considering all we've talked about this week, what is really sticking with you?

This week's big idea was Jesus's perfect life. He is the only human to obey all the way, all the time, and with all His heart.

♥ Take a moment to pause and consider how that big idea intersects with your current struggles.

Do you think you're strong enough to handle life without the Lord? Do you know you're weak and feel overwhelmed by all you lack? Do you feel like you're living on a stage? Do you feel like you're stuck behind the scenes? Do you long to be perfect? Do you feel as if you can't do anything right?

♥ Let's get specific: Where are you struggling? Where are you hungry for good news?

♥ Based on all we've learned about Jesus, what good news can you offer yourself for that place of struggle in your life?

P.S. If you can't think of something personal right now, perhaps you have a friend who is struggling in one of these areas. What good news can you offer her? You may want to use the "crying Caroline" questions to help (p. 54).

Let's close with two gospel verses. Read them over carefully so you don't overlook their good news:

For you are saved by grace through faith, and this is not from yourselves; it is God's gift—not from works, so that no one can boast.
EPHESIANS 2:8-9

Now to the one who works, pay is not credited as a gift, but as something owed. But to the one who does not work, but believes on him who justifies the ungodly, his faith is credited for righteousness.
ROMANS 4:4-5

We spend most of our time in this study talking about how the gospel is good news for our **everyday specifics.** But the gospel is also good news for our **eternal salvation.** Christ lived a perfect life to check all of the law's boxes, and when we follow Him, He takes away our sin and credits all His perfection to our account! We can't do anything to earn it, we simply trust in His work instead. When we repent and trust in Jesus, we are no longer His sin-soaked enemies but forgiven and fathered forever.

Is this something you sense the Holy Spirit is stirring in you to do? Do you desire to put yourself under God's loving leadership forever? If so, ask Him to save you! Then, tell someone who loves Jesus: "I am a Christian now!" so they can celebrate with you.

P.S. Some people feel the nudge to "get saved" a lot. But once you are God's child, you are His child forever! You don't have to keep joining the family. If you are confused about this, ask a trusted Christian leader to help you discern it. You may consider reading 1 John or John 10:27-29 together.

JESUS'S PUNISHING DEATH

SESSION 4

Group Time

> ## THIS STUDY IS ALL ABOUT GOOD NEWS!
>
> What's some good news you got this week?
>
> What's some bad news you got this week?
>
> Is there any good news hidden inside the bad news?
>
> What good news can you remember from last week's group session and study days?

INTRODUCTION

♥ We've talked about who God is—who He really is. What do you remember about that?

♥ We've also talked about sin. What do you remember about that?

Now, we get to talk about Jesus! He is Yahweh's plan to rescue the sinful world. And this rescue unfolds in three important parts, all of which are good news for you: (1) Jesus's perfect life, (2) Jesus's punishing death, and (3) Jesus's miraculous new life. Last week, we talked about Jesus's perfect life, and this week we'll talk about Jesus's punishing death.

♥ If Jesus had a perfect life, why do you think He died a punishing death? Was there anything Jesus deserved punishment for?

♥ Look up Romans 3:23 and write down the first half below. (Don't worry—we'll get to the wonderful second half of the verse soon!)

♥ Sin has been linked with death from the beginning. What evidence of death do you see in Genesis 3:21? What evidence of fatherly kindness do you see in this verse?

WATCH

As you watch the Session 4 video with your group, fill in the blanks below.

Jesus's _____wasn't a plot twist for Yahweh—it was a carefully designed _____ plan.

1. The first rescue: _____

2. The second rescue: _____

Yahweh does not leave _____ unpunished but _____ Jesus so that sinners might be_____.

His blood was shed to pay for our_____. His body was broken to cover our_____.

This is the good news of Jesus's death: It is _____ _____.

EXAMINATION

♥ With your group, read Exodus 11:4-10. What would happen in every Egyptian home if Pharaoh did not let God's people go?

♥ Verse 7 makes it clear that God's people would be safe from this terrible plague. Read Exodus 12:21-28. What did God's people need to do to be spared from death?

♥ What is dying in their place?

When John the Baptist spotted Jesus at the beginning of His ministry, He exclaimed, "Look, the Lamb of God, who takes away the sin of the world!" (John 1:29).

♥ Why does John call Jesus "the Lamb of God"? What connections can you make between the Passover lamb in Exodus 12 and Jesus?

♥ Last week, we talked about how Jesus lived the perfect life. He certainly didn't deserve a punishing death! Whose sin deserves death?

Remembering our desperate sin problem is crucial. Matthew Barrett says, "It's only when we come to terms with our own utter unworthiness, inability, and depravity that we can even begin to understand why it was so necessary for God to become man."[1] We needed God to save us oh so badly!

This leaves us with one remaining question: Why? If Jesus didn't deserve to die, why did He? Of course, we needed Him, but He had no obligation to rescue people who continually rejected His ways. So why even go to all the trouble?

Let's see what Scripture has to say about this. One great way to pay better attention when you read the Bible is to look for repeated words and ideas.

♥ **What word or idea do you see repeated in the following collection of verses?**

> *"For God loved the world in this way: He gave his one and only Son, so that everyone who believes in him will not perish but have eternal life."*
> JOHN 3:16

> *Before the Passover Festival, Jesus knew that his hour had come to depart from this world to the Father. Having loved his own who were in the world, he loved them to the end.*
> JOHN 13:1

> *"No one has greater love than this: to lay down his life for his friends."*
> JOHN 15:13

So, if Jesus didn't deserve to die, why did He?

Jesus is described as the Passover lamb, but interestingly, Jesus also describes Himself as the Good Shepherd. You probably don't know many shepherds and aren't as familiar with the profession as people were in Jesus's day, so here's an overview: The work of a shepherd was characterized by constant care and sacrifice. The shepherd—a good one, anyway—always kept watch, always provided for the needs of the sheep, and always faced the sheep's enemies, even if it cost him his life.

♥ **Read John 10:11-15 below. As you read:**

1. **Circle the word *shepherd* every time you see it.**

2. **Underline anything the shepherd does.**

> [11] *"I am the good shepherd. The good shepherd lays down his life for the sheep.* [12] *The hired hand, since he is not the shepherd and doesn't own the sheep, leaves them and runs away when he sees a wolf coming. The wolf then snatches and scatters them.* [13] *This happens because he is a hired hand and doesn't care about the sheep.*

¹⁴ "I am the good shepherd. I know my own, and my own know me, ¹⁵ just as the Father knows me, and I know the Father. I lay down my life for the sheep."

♥ Is there anything in this passage that reminds you of the way God described sin in Genesis 4:7?

Others you know may be like the hired hand—afraid to deal with your sin, loving their life more than yours, choosing what is easy for them over what is rescuing for you. But Jesus is not like the hired hand. Jesus is not like anyone you know! He is the Good Shepherd, and because He loves His sheep, He is willing to take on the devouring enemy of sin, even though it cost Him His own life.

APPLICATION

We've related Jesus's punishing death to general sin, but Jesus's punishing death is good news for your specific sin.

Here's a question to consider in your own mind and not with your group: Can you think of something you've done that makes you want to hide? Something that causes you deep shame and embarrassment when you think of it?

It's painful, but we want to put the good news of the gospel exactly where it hurts, so that you can experience life in places that feel like death.

♥ Take a minute or two, close your eyes, and ponder a specific sin that grieves you. You can journal below if that's helpful.

_____
_____
_____
_____
_____
_____
_____

♥ Now, together with you group, answer these questions:

1. Is the Good Shepherd afraid to face that sin?

2. What is the Good Shepherd willing to do so that you won't be devoured because of that sin?

3. Why is the Good Shepherd willing to lay down His life?

4. Is this sin covered?

5. Do you believe this sin is truly covered?

6. How might your life be different if you truly believed that this sin is covered by the blood of Jesus?

PRAY

Close in prayer, praising God for the good news of the gospel and asking Him to help you and your group to grasp it in a deeper way.

Good News for When You Know You're Bad and for When You're Worried God Isn't Good

Being a human is hard. There are days when you are so deeply convinced of your sinfulness that it's difficult to cope.

There are days when God seems so uncaring.

> If He's actually loving, why isn't He _____?

> (Go ahead and fill in that blank with whatever it seems He isn't doing.)

When our thoughts and feelings seem to be wrapped in barbed wire, it can be difficult to navigate through them without getting injured.

Did you know that two other people were crucified next to Jesus? It's a detail we sometimes overlook, but the story of these men offers good news for the girl who knows she's bad—and for the girl who worries God isn't good.

♥ Read Luke 23:32-43. As you do, feel free to make notes below or in the margins of anything you notice about this passage. Write down any details that tell you about the characters of the men crucified next to Jesus.

Let's pay attention to the words the people in this scene said to one another.

♥ What did those crucifying Jesus say to Him? What was their tone?

♥ What did Jesus say to God about those who were crucifying Him? What was His tone towards them?

♥ The two men being crucified next to Jesus spoke to Him differently. What did the first man say? The second man?

♥ How did Jesus respond?

With this story in mind, consider the following questions:

♥ How does Jesus respond to people who are inarguably bad?

♥ What does that say about God's goodness?

♥ How can you remember this the next time you know you are bad? What does Jesus's death mean for your sin?

♥ How can you remember this the next time you wonder if He's actually good? How does Jesus's posture towards sinners impact you?

Good News for When You Feel Ashamed and for When You Feel Nothing

I've been a Christian for a long time, but I still struggle to understand the gospel is true. Shame can grow big in my heart, and I become just like Eve, clumsily seeking to cover up with fig leaves or foolishly trying to hide where Yahweh cannot find me. Other times, I feel nothing at all. My sin doesn't bother me, and everything seems pointless. Can you relate?

In those moments of severe shame or total numbness, I want to give you a verse to look to.

♥ Read Psalm 34:8 then follow the prompts below.

1. Circle the words *taste* and *good*. These are for the girl who feels nothing. Who is the source of goodness? _____

2. Then, underline the words *happy* and *refuge*. These are for the girl who feels shame. Who is the source of the happiness? _____

3. To help us think of these words in light of the gospel, particularly the part we're studying this week (Jesus's punishing death), read Luke 22:19-20. In your Bible, circle the two times Jesus says, "for you."

Jesus and His disciples were celebrating Passover, that time long-ago when death passed over God's people because their doorposts were covered with the blood of a perfect lamb. Let's think about Passover and the Last Supper in light of Psalm 34:8a.

> *Taste and see that the LORD is good.*
> PSALM 34:8a

Passover: After the Passover event, God's people were instructed to have the Passover meal every year to help them remember. Imagine the first families to celebrate Passover, who were able to do so with their firstborn children who would've died if it were not for the blood of the lamb.

♥ Their taste buds probably enjoyed this shared meal, but how did its good taste likely go deeper than mere flavor?

The Last Supper: At church, we often take communion or the Lord's Supper. We remember Jesus's words that His body was broken and His blood was poured out for us.

♥ How does the goodness of this go deeper than mere flavor?

Now let's think about Passover and the Last Supper in light of Psalm 34:8b.

How happy is the person who takes refuge in him!
PSALM 34:8b

Passover: Imagine what it was like to go to sleep the night death was supposed to visit every house.

♥ How did the blood of the lamb offer refuge? (*Refuge* means "shelter or protection from danger or distress."[2]) When dawn came, how do you imagine those covered by the blood felt?

The Last Supper: The Bible is clear that sin deserves death, and it's clear that all are sinners. Our deserved fate is obvious. But at the Last Supper, Jesus is clear about the purpose of His blood.

♥ Who is it poured out for? How is His blood a refuge for sinners? When judgment comes, how do you imagine those covered by the blood will feel?

Feeling nothing is part of life in this broken world, and yet God can use the gospel to allow our spiritual taste buds to come alive. It's true: God offers your soul the spiritual food you've been craving—Himself! He is yours by the blood of the Lamb.

Feeling shame is part of life in this broken world, and yet God can use the gospel to replace our shame with sheer happiness. It's true: You do not have to hide, but are hidden in Him! All your shameful deeds are covered by the blood of the Lamb.

When the good news doesn't feel true, it's still true:

He was exposed that you might be covered.

He was killed that you might have life.

He endured shame that you might know you're loved.

He bore your sin that you might have His righteousness.

He was injured that you might be healed.

Good News for When You Hate Your Body and for When You Want Others to Notice Your Body

The gospel has transformed the way I view my body. I know it sounds crazy. Can the gospel actually offer good news for the girl who hates her body and for the girl who wants others to notice her body? Trust me: The gospel can transform your relationship with the mirror and calm that deep "notice me" craving.

Let's touch on a few of the gospel elements we've encountered so far to see what they have to say about our bodies:

GOD

♥ Look up Genesis 1:26 and answer the following:

1. Who made the human body?

2. In whose image did He make human bodies?

♥ Read Psalm 139:13-16 and answer the following:

1. In verse 14, circle two words that describe the way God made the human body.

2. Look these two words up in a dictionary. What do they mean?

3. Who knit you together in your mother's womb?

4. What do all of these things mean about your body's value to God?

5. Does He value your body because you've shaped it a certain way or because He's shaped it?

SIN

♥ Sin impacts bodies and the ways we think about our bodies. Look up Genesis 4:7. How does God describe sin?

♥ How has sin impacted your body? How has sin impacted the way you feel about your body?

JESUS

The idea of incarnation teaches us that God himself came to live in human flesh.

♥ Read Mark 11:12 and John 4:6. How do we see Jesus's humanity in these verses?

Jesus understands the limitations and difficulties of the human body, and yet He willingly took them on and endured some of the most horrific emotional, physical, and spiritual suffering imaginable.

♥ Read Luke 22:39-44. What was Jesus's body experiencing as He knew His crucifixion was approaching?

♥ Read Luke 22:63-65. Write down what Jesus was experiencing.

♥ Based on what you know about the crucifixion, what kind of things did Jesus endure while He was dying?

♥ Read Hebrews 12:2. Why did Jesus endure these things?

What was "the joy that lay before him"? It was the one thing that Yahweh did not have—true togetherness with His children. He doesn't need us, but He wants us! He loves us so much that He endured the cross. The joy set before Him is you, me, and our spiritual siblings.

♥ How could this, if you truly believed it, change the way you see yourself and your body?

If you want a practical tool to help you view your body in light of the gospel, check out my "mirror mantra" on page 140.

Have you ever looked in a magnifying mirror? Things might seem fine at first, but soon every single pore starts to look disgusting. It's overwhelming! I usually come away from a magnifying mirror wishing I could vacuum out my face or just get a new one.

Magnifying mirrors have taught me that we were not designed to behold ourselves. When we fix our gaze on ourselves, we despair. We begin to hate our bodies, desire for others to love our bodies, or both.

But when we behold Jesus, we see ourselves differently:

God: We know our bodies were shaped carefully by a good Creator.

Sin: We know that sin is at work in and around us, but that Jesus is the ultimate victor over sin.

Jesus: We know that His body endured death so that we might have life.

All of these little gospel nuggets begin, over time, to form a satisfying feast. As we are careful to fix our gaze on Him and let that inform how we interact with the mirror, as we sing the gospel over ourselves in fittings rooms and at pool parties, He shapes our insides in a way that is good news for our outsides.

♥ Write a sentence describing a gospel-informed way to view your body:

Sister, behold the right body. And then look at yours. It will change everything.

Discovery

GOOD NEWS FOR WHEN YOU_____

♥ Take a few minutes and flip through this week's study pages. Considering all we've talked about this week, what is really sticking with you?

This week's big idea was Jesus's punishing death. He endured death so that we might have life. He was exposed and shamed that we might be covered and cherished. Wow.

♥ Take a moment to pause and consider how that big idea intersects with your current struggles.

Are you struggling because you know you're bad? Or maybe because you suspect God isn't good? Are you struggling because you feel overcome with shame? Or maybe because you feel nothing at all when it comes to your sin? Are you struggling because you hate your body? Or maybe because you long for someone else to praise your body? Something else entirely? Basically, let's get specific:

♥ Where are you struggling? Where are you hungry for good news?

♥ Based on all we've learned about Jesus, what good news can you offer yourself for that place of struggle in your life? (If you can't think of something personal right now, perhaps you have a friend who is struggling in one of these areas. What good news can you offer her?)

Let's close with two gospel verses. Read them over carefully so you don't overlook their good news:

**For God was pleased to have all his fullness dwell
in him, and through him to reconcile everything to
himself, whether things on earth or things in heaven, by
making peace through his blood, shed on the cross.**
COLOSSIANS 1:19-20

**Adopt the same attitude as that of Christ Jesus, who,
existing in the form of God, did not consider equality
with God as something to be exploited. Instead he
emptied himself by assuming the form of a servant, taking
on the likeness of humanity. And when he had come
as a man, he humbled himself by becoming obedient
to the point of death—even to death on a cross.**
PHILIPPIANS 2:5-8

We spend most of our time in this study talking about how the gospel is good news for our **everyday specifics.** But the gospel is also good news for our **eternal salvation.** These verses teach us that God was pleased to have His fullness dwell in the person of Jesus and that Jesus served at great cost, making a way for humans to be reunited with God and at peace with Him. He endured the cross because of a simple but hard to believe truth: He loves you. When we recognize that our staggering sinfulness and God's tremendous love made the cross necessary, we can repent and trust in Jesus. Then we are no longer His sin-soaked enemies but forgiven and fathered forever.

Is this something you sense the Holy Spirit is stirring in you to do? Do you desire to put yourself under God's loving leadership forever? If so, ask Him to save you! Then, tell someone who loves Jesus: "I am a Christian now!" so they can celebrate with you.

P.S. Some people feel the nudge to "get saved" a lot. But once you are God's child, you are His child forever! You don't have to keep joining the family. If you are confused about this, ask a trusted Christian leader to help you discern it. You may consider reading 1 John or John 10:27-29 together.

JESUS'S
NEW LIFE

SESSION 5

Group time

THIS STUDY IS ALL ABOUT GOOD NEWS!

What's some good news you got this week?

What's some bad news you got this week?

Is there any good news hidden inside the bad news?

What good news can you remember from last week's group session and study days?

INTRODUCTION

If we're honest, everything we've covered so far is a little wild to wrap our minds around.

♥ We've talked about God, sin, and Jesus—how He lived the perfect life no one could live and how He died a punishing death in our place. What about these things has been difficult to wrap your mind around?

♥ What is something you've learned that has blown your mind?

The good news we'll talk about today is potentially the wildest part: the part where Jesus miraculously defeats death by coming back to life.

♥ Why do you think people have always struggled to believe this part?

GROUP DISCUSSION

♥ Read John 20:24-29. Why did Thomas struggle to believe Jesus was truly alive?

♥ Look up Jeremiah 32:27. What was Thomas likely forgetting?

♥ Read John 20:11-16. Make a list of things Mary sees in this "scene."

WATCH

As you watch the Session 5 video with your group, fill in the blanks below.

When we follow _____, instead of the death we _____, we receive new _____.

Jesus's _____ is a phenomenal act of _____.

The _____ seat was a _____ for sin.

Because Jesus conquered the grave:

1. You do not have to fear _____ or anything that feels like _____.

2. You can experience resurrection _____ in all kinds of _____.

3. You can _____ with _____.

EXAMINATION

♥ Look up the verses below, then attempt to draw what was described in each box.

Exodus 25:10-22	John 20:11-12

♥ What similarities do you notice between the two drawings?

♥ Try to remember all the things you've learned about Yahweh, and consider this: Do you think Yahweh knew about the events described in John 20 when He was giving Moses the tabernacle instructions in Exodus 25? What characteristic does Yahweh have that helps you answer that question? (Hint: Remember CLUPS.)

Exodus 25:22 says, "I will meet with you there above the mercy seat." If you look up the term *mercy seat* in an original language dictionary, you'll see its definition is "propitiatory."[1] (Side note: Don't you hate it when a dictionary gives you a definition that's harder than the word?)

♥ Let's use some other parts of Scripture to help us understand this word. Circle any word similar to "propitiatory":

> *He is the propitiation for our sins, and not for ours only*
> *but also for the sins of the whole world.*
> 1 JOHN 2:2, ESV

> *In this is love, not that we have loved God but that he loved us*
> *and sent his Son to be the propitiation for our sins.*
> 1 JOHN 4:10, ESV

♥ According to these verses, who is the propitiation for our sins?

Propitiatory/propitiation means "averting the wrath of God by the offering of a gift."[2] After studying this word a bit, I think you can put it this way: "a covering for sin."[3]

♥ What is required for sin to be covered?

♥ What did Jesus do to be the "propitiation for our sins"?

♥ Jesus is our true mercy seat! Look up Exodus 25:22 again. What does this verse help us see about Jesus?

APPLICATION

We've talked generally about the good news of Jesus's miraculous new life, but let's get specific:

♥ Do you ever fear death? (It can be your own death or the death of another person.) What seems scary about this? (If you don't battle this fear, try to imagine why others fear it.)

♥ Let's talk about death in a more figurative sense. What are some losses or longings that a person might fear or grieve in a death-like way?

In C.S. Lewis's book *The Lion, the Witch, and the Wardrobe*, the Jesus figure, Aslan, comes back to life after laying down his life for a traitor. Does the passage below—especially the underlined part—help you understand how exciting Jesus's power over death truly is?

> There, shining in the sunrise, larger than they had seen him before, shaking his mane (for it had apparently grown again) stood Aslan himself.
>
> "Oh, Aslan!" cried both the children, staring up at him, almost as much frightened as they were glad . . . .
>
> "But what does it all mean?" asked Susan when they were somewhat calmer.
>
> "It means," said Aslan, "that though the Witch knew the Deep Magic, there is a magic deeper still which she did not know. Her knowledge goes back only to the dawn of time. But if she could have looked a little further back, into the stillness and the darkness before Time dawned, she would have read there a different incantation. <u>She would have known that when a willing victim who had committed no treachery was killed in a traitor's stead, the Table would crack and Death itself would start working backward.</u>"[4]

♥ The Bible is clear: God is stronger than death. God has power over death. Skim the following passages and write down the big event that happened in each:

Genesis 2:7,22	
Ezekiel 37:1-10	

1 Kings 17:17-24	
2 Kings 4:32-35	
Luke 7:11-17	
Luke 8:51-56	
John 11:38-44	

♥ When death (literal or figurative) overwhelms you, how can you remind yourself of God's power over death?

The good news of Jesus's resurrection shows more than God's power over death—it also shows His love!

♥ Explain the connection between Jesus's power over death and His love for us. (Hint: Think about the mercy seat and what had to occur for God to meet with us.)

♥ Is it hard for you to believe that Jesus loves you? Tell me about it.

♥ When death (literal or figurative) overwhelms you, how can you remind yourself of God's love for you?

PRAY

Close in prayer, praising God for the good news of the gospel and asking Him to help you and your group to grasp it in a deeper way.

Good News for When You Don't Understand What God Is Doing

All Christians have seasons in which we wonder, "Lord, what are you doing?" This question especially tends to shove its way in when death, sickness, and loss occur.

♥   Read John 11:1-7,11-19 below. As you read:

1.   Underline every instance sickness or death is mentioned.

2.   Circle every instance you see time mentioned.

3.   Double underline any details that might make people (like the disciples, Mary, or Martha) wonder, "Lord, what are you doing?"

1 Now a man was sick, Lazarus from Bethany, the village of Mary and her sister Martha. 2 Mary was the one who anointed the Lord with perfume and wiped his feet with her hair, and it was her brother Lazarus who was sick. 3 So the sisters sent a message to him: "Lord, the one you love is sick." 4 When Jesus heard it, he said, "This sickness will not end in death but is for the glory of God, so that the Son of God may be glorified through it." 5 Now Jesus loved Martha, her sister, and Lazarus. 6 So when he heard that he was sick, he stayed two more days in the place where he was. 7 Then after that, he said to the disciples, "Let's go to Judea again."

. . .

11 He told them, "Our friend Lazarus has fallen asleep, but I'm on my way to wake him up." 12 Then the disciples said to him, "Lord, if he has fallen asleep, he will get well." 13 Jesus, however, was speaking about his death, but they thought he was speaking about natural sleep. 14 So Jesus then told them plainly, "Lazarus has died. 15 I'm glad for you that I wasn't there so that you may believe. But let's go to him." 16 Then Thomas (called "Twin") said to his fellow disciples, "Let's go too so that we may die with him." 17 When Jesus arrived, he found that Lazarus had already been in the tomb four days. 18 Bethany was near Jerusalem (less than two miles away). 19 Many of the Jews had come to Martha and Mary to comfort them about their brother.

♥ Let's observe the text a little bit more. Answer the questions below, and include the reference where you found the answer.

1. How did Jesus feel about Lazarus?

2. Did Lazarus die?

3. Did Jesus immediately go to help his friends Mary, Martha, and Lazarus? What did He do?

4. Jewish tradition held that the soul lingers near the body for three days after death.[5] How long was Lazarus in the tomb?

5. After days of grieving their brother and not hearing from Jesus, how do you imagine Mary and Martha felt?

6. Look at everything you double-underlined and then read verses 4 and 14-15. How do these verses help you understand (a) why Lazarus died and (b) why Jesus responded to Lazarus's death the way He did?

7. Now that we've observed the passage more closely, how do you think Jesus would answer the question, "Lord, what are you doing?"

8. Remember, Yahweh never changes. The God you see in this passage is the same God you know! How does this offer you hope?

PERSONAL STUDY 2

Good News for When You Doubt Who God Is

When our circumstances are favorable, it's easier to believe God is good. But when they aren't, we're prone to doubt.

♥ Think about what we learned about God in the first session. Does He ever change? What do you know to be true about Him?

♥ Read John 11:20-32 below. As you read:

1. Underline everything Martha tells us about Jesus.

2. Double underline everything Jesus tells us about Himself.

> [20] As soon as Martha heard that Jesus was coming, she went to meet him, but Mary remained seated in the house. [21] Then Martha said to Jesus, "Lord, if you had been here, my brother wouldn't have died. [22] Yet even now I know that whatever you ask from God, God will give you." [23] "Your brother will rise again," Jesus told her. [24] Martha said to him, "I know that he will rise again in the resurrection at the last day." [25] Jesus said to her, "I am the resurrection and the life. The one who believes in me, even if he dies, will live. [26] Everyone who lives and believes in me will never die. Do you believe this?" [27] "Yes, Lord," she told him, "I believe you are the Messiah, the Son of God, who comes into the world." [28] Having said this, she went back and called her sister Mary, saying in private, "The Teacher is here and is calling for you." [29] As soon as Mary heard this, she got up quickly and went to him. [30] Jesus had not yet come into the village but was still in the place where Martha had met him. [31] The Jews who were with her in the house consoling her saw that Mary got up quickly and went out. They followed her, supposing that she was going to the tomb to cry there. [32] As soon as Mary came to where Jesus was and saw him, she fell at his feet and told him, "Lord, if you had been here, my brother wouldn't have died!"

♥ Let's observe the text a bit more. Answer the following questions:

1. What do Mary and Martha both say to Jesus when they first see Him?

2. Martha declares an important spiritual truth in verse 24, telling Jesus that she knows Lazarus will rise again in the resurrection. (We'll talk more about in Session 7.) She's certain this God-promised event, the resurrection, is real. And yet, how does Jesus gently prompt her to believe in a bigger way in verse 25?

3. Fill in the blanks: "_____ _____ the resurrection and the life." What do you think this means?

♥ Look up the following verses. What do they tell you about Jesus and life?

John 1:4	
John 3:16	
John 6:35	
John 10:10	
John 14:6	

Life is offered eternally to Jesus's followers, and it's offered every day! How? He is life, so to have Him is to have life!

♥ When something feels like death, what are some "life-giving" qualities or stories about the Lord that you can remember? Make a list.

♥ Pray and ask Jesus right now to prompt you to believe in a deeper way.

P.S. Sometimes "believing more" feels impossible. We are too crushed, heartbroken, numb, or angry. (Look up Mark 9:24 and Luke 17:5 for short prayers to pray.) Though Jesus responded to Martha's grief by inviting her to believe in a deeper way, He responds differently to her sister Mary. Stay tuned!

Good News for When You're Grieving

Jesus responded to Martha's grief by gently prompting her to believe in a deeper way, but He responded differently to Mary.

♥ Read John 11:33-45 below. As you read:

1. Underline anything that indicates emotion in Mary.

2. Double underline anything that indicates emotion in Jesus.

3. Put an exclamation point above anything startling.

> [33] *When Jesus saw her crying, and the Jews who had come with her crying, he was deeply moved in his spirit and troubled.* [34] *"Where have you put him?" he asked. "Lord," they told him, "come and see."* [35] *Jesus wept.* [36] *So the Jews said, "See how he loved him!"* [37] *But some of them said, "Couldn't he who opened the blind man's eyes also have kept this man from dying?"* [38] *Then Jesus, deeply moved again, came to the tomb. It was a cave, and a stone was lying against it.* [39] *"Remove the stone," Jesus said. Martha, the dead man's sister, told him, "Lord, there is already a stench because he has been dead four days."* [40] *Jesus said to her, "Didn't I tell you that if you believed you would see the glory of God?"* [41] *So they removed the stone. Then Jesus raised his eyes and said, "Father, I thank you that you heard me.* [42] *I know that you always hear me, but because of the crowd standing here I said this, so that they may believe you sent me."* [43] *After he said this, he shouted with a loud voice, "Lazarus, come out!"* [44] *The dead man came out bound hand and foot with linen strips and with his face wrapped in a cloth. Jesus said to them, "Unwrap him and let him go."* [45] *Therefore, many of the Jews who came to Mary and saw what he did believed in him.*

I mean, WOW! This story!

♥ Let's observe the text a bit more closely by answering the following questions:

1. Consider the emotion we've seen in Mary. How does Jesus respond to her?

2. In what two ways do the Jews respond to Jesus's tears?

3. How does verse 45 fulfill what Jesus said in verses 4 and 14-15?

4. How does verse 44 fulfill what Jesus said in verse 25?

In verse 39, Jesus is about to do something amazing, but Martha interrupts, worried about a smell. This woman is always thinking, always practical. (I love her.) I think that's why Jesus often appealed to her theology! In verse 40, Jesus again invites Martha to deeper belief. He can tell she doesn't believe as fully as she thinks she does! Isn't it a little funny how she says she believes Jesus is God but doesn't seem to believe He knows decaying bodies have an odor? That she believes He has power over death but not power over stench?

♥ Do you ever notice "little disbeliefs" like that in your life? Tell me about it.

This story has two important themes: belief and grief. Let's look at both:

BELIEF

Look over this week's readings from John 11 and put a star above any mention of belief. What connections can you make? Use the space below to journal a bit.

GRIEF

Look again and put a sad face above anything related to grief. John 11:35 is well-known as the shortest verse in the Bible, yet it carries tremendous impact. How might these tears minister to you when you are tearful?

I first read *The Magician's Nephew* by C.S. Lewis in the fourth grade, but I recently read it as an adult, and I was captivated by Aslan (the Jesus figure) and his tears. No doubt Lewis was inspired by John 11 when he penned this passage about a little boy whose mother is very sick:

> "But please, please—won't you—can't you give me something that will cure Mother?'
> Up till then he had been looking at the Lion's great feet and the huge claws on
> them; now, in his despair, he looked up at its face. What he saw surprised him as
> much as anything in his whole life. For the tawny face was bent down near his own
> and (wonder of wonders) great shining tears stood in the Lion's eyes. They were
> such big, bright tears compared with Digory's own that for a moment he felt as if
> the Lion must really be sorrier about his Mother than he was himself.
>
> 'My son, my son,' said Aslan. 'I know. Grief is great.'"[6]

Jesus wept because He knows the horror and devastation of death! Though we may long for Jesus to literally resurrect someone, that is likely not how He will care for us in our grief. And yet, the person of Jesus that we see so vividly in this story is true for you, true for your family. His character never changes!

And that, dear sister, is why He Himself came to conquer it. He mourns with you when you grieve, and He defeated it so that His followers may have life.

Do you believe?

Discovery

GOOD NEWS FOR WHEN YOU_____

♥ Take a few minutes and flip through this week's study pages. Considering all we've talked about this week, what is really sticking with you?

This week's big idea was Jesus's new life. The resurrection is good news in an Easter way ("He is risen! He is risen indeed!"), but it is also good news in an everyday way.

♥ Take a moment and examine your heart. Where are you struggling? Where are you hungry for good news? Are you struggling because you don't understand what God is doing, because you doubt who God is, because you are grieving? What feels like death to you?

♥ Based on all we've learned about Jesus, what good news can you offer yourself for that place of struggle in your life? (If you can't think of something personal right now, perhaps you have a friend who is struggling in one of these areas. What good news can you offer her?)

Let's close with two gospel verses. Read them over carefully so you don't overlook their good news:

But God, who is rich in mercy, because of his great love that he had for us, made us alive with Christ even though we were dead in trespasses. You are saved by grace!
EPHESIANS 2:4-5

"Truly I tell you, anyone who hears my word and believes him who sent me has eternal life and will not come under judgment but has passed from death to life."
JOHN 5:24

We spend most of our time in this study talking about how the gospel is good news for our **everyday specifics.** But the gospel is also good news for our **eternal salvation.** These verses remind us that Jesus's new life becomes our new life when we follow Him! Sin is an enemy that kills, but Jesus conquered it on the cross by being killed Himself, and then conquered death itself by being raised to life. If you hear His gospel and believe it—that you're a sinner, that Jesus bore your sin, that He lives and so you can too—then you are no longer His sin-soaked enemies but forgiven and fathered forever.

Are you sensing the Holy Spirit is stirring in you to repent and follow Jesus? Do you desire to put yourself under God's loving leadership forever? If so, ask Him to save you! Then, tell someone who loves Jesus: "I am a Christian now!" so they can celebrate with you.

P.S. Some people feel the nudge to "get saved" a lot. But once you are God's child, you are His child forever! You don't have to keep joining the family. If you are confused about this, ask a trusted Christian leader to help you discern it. You may consider reading 1 John or John 10:27-29 together.

THE HOLY SPIRIT

SESSION 6

Group time

THIS STUDY IS ALL ABOUT GOOD NEWS!

What's some good news you got this week?

What's some bad news you got this week?

Is there any good news hidden inside the bad news?

What good news can you remember from last week's group session and study days?

INTRODUCTION

Depending on your background, some people might be more familiar with the Holy Spirit than others.

♥ What do you know about the Holy Spirit?

Let's look at what Jesus said about the Holy Spirit:

♥ At the Last Supper, Jesus talked a lot about the Holy Spirit. Read John 14:16-17,26 and John 16:7-15 and make a list of things Jesus taught about the Holy Spirit:

♥ Before He ascended to heaven, Jesus talked about the Holy Spirit. Read Acts 1:1-11 and make a list of things Jesus taught about the Holy Spirit:

♥ Let's look at what happened the first time the Spirit came to live within God's people. Read Acts 2:1-11,37-41 and list at least three big things that happened:

WATCH

As you watch the Session 6 video with your group, fill in the blanks below.

God is one God, and yet God _____ has three distinct persons: the _____, the _____, and the _____ _____.

Perfect _____ is always at _____ within God the Father, God the Son, and God the Spirit.

If you are a Jesus _____, the Holy Spirit is within _____, helping _____ in every way.

We are new _____ in Christ, but we don't _____ grow Spirit fruit.

EXAMINATION

The Holy Spirit has lots of jobs, and I like to list them with 7 Cs. (This is not a comprehensive list. The Holy Spirit does so much!) Have a volunteer in your group read this out loud, and as she reads, circle the "C" word in each sentence.

1. The Holy Spirit **convicts** God's people of their sin, reminding them it's a big deal, so they can repent and change.

2. The Holy Spirit helps God's people **combat** their sin, so they can have victory over it.

3. The Holy Spirit **comforts** God's people with God's presence, reminding them they are not alone, reminding them that they are forever in His family.

4. The Holy Spirit **counsels** God's people to understand and follow God's Word, showing them how to follow God in the most confusing places.

5. The Holy Spirit **connects** God's people with one another, creating a family that lasts forever.

6. The Holy Spirit **communicates** God's works through God's people, so that others may follow Him, too!

7. The Holy Spirit **crafts** God's people from the inside, so that they can grow and become more like God.

♥ Which of the 7 Cs surprises you?

♥ Which of the 7 Cs feels like especially good news?

♥ Check out these verses in the book of Acts (when the Holy Spirit first gets to work in God's people). How do you see the Holy Spirit at work? (Feel free to use one of the "C" words.)

Acts 2:37	
Acts 7:54-60	
Acts 8:29	
Acts 9:31	

APPLICATION

We are God's daughters from the moment we are spiritually born into His family. But as He parents us and is near us, we begin to look more like Him on the inside.

What good news that God doesn't say, "Okay, great! You're my kid now! Figure your life out, and I'll see you in heaven!" Instead, He's with us, teaches us, and helps us grow to be more like Him.

In Galatians 5, Paul writes to the church at Galatia about two different kinds of fruit: (1) "flesh fruit"—the fruit we grow when we are following ourselves, and (2) "Spirit fruit"—the fruit we grow when we are following the Spirit.

♥ Read the list of "flesh fruit" in verses 19-21. (Pretty gross, right?) You may want to look up or discuss what some of them mean. (For example, selfish ambition is when a person puts herself, what she wants, and who she wants to be above everything and everyone else.)

♥ Read verses 22-23. Isn't this list a relief?

♥ This word "fruit" is singular. It's not like there's lots of "Spirit fruit"— there's one, and it's got a lot of flavors. Write out the different flavors of Spirit fruit below:

In theory, a person filled with God's Spirit will always grow Spirit fruit, the way apple trees always grow apples. But people aren't exactly like trees. In the life of a Christian, flesh fruit can still grow up like weeds, but the Holy Spirit can help us kill it! When it comes to Spirit fruit, God is the grower, but we have to be willing "soil." Let's dig into that:

♥ Read Galatians 5:16,25. God is the ultimate grower, but what might it look like to be willing "soil"?

Earlier, we looked at what Jesus said about the Holy Spirit at the Last Supper. At this dinner, Jesus also talked about fruit.

- ♥ Read John 15:4-5. How can we be willing soil for Jesus fruit?

- ♥ "Spirit fruit" and "Jesus fruit" are weird, made-up terms that mean the same thing: God is growing godliness in you! Can you think of someone you know who seems to have "God-flavored" fruit growing in their life?

- ♥ What kinds of habits might a person try to develop if she wants God to grow Spirit fruit in her life?

- ♥ Read Galatians 5:16-18. The Spirit and the flesh are _____ to each other.

The battle between "Spirit fruit" v. "flesh fruit" was a big problem for me in middle and high school (and even now, sometimes!) when it came to being liked. I was a Christian, and I wanted to follow God with my whole heart, but I also wanted to be popular—even if that meant I had to talk or act in ways that were the opposite of God's character. The "flesh fruit" of selfish ambition was growing like a weed! I didn't understand the good news of the Holy Spirit:

- *I knew He was doing His job of **convicting** me of sin, but I thought He just wanted me to be a good girl. I didn't realize sin was a dangerous enemy, and His conviction is like a parent cautioning a kid to avoid the neighbor's mean, biting dog.*

- *I didn't understand the Spirit would **comfort** me with God's presence, so I would know I'm never alone, so I could know I am God's daughter forever—eternally liked and loved—even when I mess up.*

- *I didn't understand He would help me **combat** this sin. I thought it was just my fight.*

- *I didn't understand that He could **connect** me with other God followers who could help me and remind me what's true.*

- *I didn't understand that He was using all of this to **craft** my insides to match the new creation I was in Christ.*

This is a miracle you could only fully grasp if you lived inside my head at thirteen years old: Because of God at work in my life, I am so delighted by the approval I have from my Father in heaven. Because of Jesus, the approval of people simply doesn't matter as much to me! Spirit fruit is growing slow (and it needs to grow more!), but it is definitely growing. God can do this in you, too!

♥ Is there an area in your life where you are struggling in the battle of "Spirit fruit" v. "flesh fruit" and need to be reminded of the good news of the Holy Spirit?

♥ Read Galatians 5:24-26. What needs to be done to the flesh? Based on what you've learned in this study, who can help you do that?

♥ Why should we not become conceited about the "Spirit fruit" that grows in our lives?

Remember what Jesus said about fruit in John 15:4-5? It grows when we're with Him. That means, we grow Spirit fruit by staying in active relationship with God. Galatians 5:25 calls this "keeping in step with the Spirit."

Think about it: When you are in active relationship with a friend (seeing her all the time, talking to her a lot, getting her advice, etc.), you will begin to act, talk, and think like your friend.

♥ What do you think it might look like to be in an active relationship with God?

Sister, go with God! Shape your life around Him, and let Him work within you. You will be amazed to look back and see how flesh fruit has died while Spirit fruit grows and grows. It's all a delicious miracle from our Good Grower!

PRAY

Close in prayer, praising God for the good news of the gospel and asking Him to help you and your group to grasp it in a deeper way.

Good News for When You Feel All Alone

The Holy Spirit is good news when you feel all alone because He comforts and connects. Check out the charts below:

1. Look up each verse in the first column and match the reference with its truth and the way it describes the Holy Spirit.

John 14:26	Truth 1: The Holy Spirit is with us forever.
Romans 8:16	Truth 2: The Holy Spirit reminds us of God's truth.
John 14:16	Truth 3: The Holy Spirit assures us we are God's children.

2. Then, complete the chart.

	How does it comfort?	How does it connect?
Truth 1		
Truth 2		
Truth 3		

Though we may feel alone, we aren't! We have the most loving Father imaginable who is with us every moment—plus a gigantic family of believers. Of course, these things aren't functioning perfectly all the time. That won't happen until Jesus returns. (Aren't you excited about next session?)

Let's take a look at a passage Paul wrote to the church in Corinth. Paul and the Christians there had endured some prickly, painful conflict. As you read Paul's words, remember Paul and the Corinthians are probably a lot like you right now: desiring comfort and connection.

♥ Read 2 Corinthians 1:3-4 on the next page. Circle anything you see about comfort, and underline anything you see about connection.

[3] Blessed be the God and Father of our Lord Jesus Christ, the Father of mercies and the God of all comfort. [4] He comforts us in all our affliction, so that we may be able to comfort those who are in any kind of affliction, through the comfort we ourselves receive from God.

♥ Let's observe the text a bit more closely:

1. In verse 3, who does Paul say is the source of ALL comfort? (Double-underline the word "all" in the verse.)

2. Affliction is something that causes pain or distress.[1] Who comforts us when we are afflicted?

3. When you see the words "so that" in Scripture, it's like saying, "Here's why." Read the passage again with that in mind. Why does God comfort us in our affliction?

4. Look at the last part of verse 4. What do we use to comfort others?

5. Remember the Holy Spirit helps craft us to look more like God. In this passage, what specific trait of God's character do we see Him handing down to His children?

6. Romans 8:28 assures us God works all things together for good for His children. Affliction never feels good, but how does God use it for good?

God's comfort is designed to be contagious! When we are comforted by Him, inevitably, there will be an opportunity to extend that same comfort to others, and in the process, that person will be comforted, and we will become more like God, the ultimate Comforter.

♥ Have you ever had a time when you received comfort from the Lord and were able to share it with someone else? How did that experience increase your connection with that person? With the Lord?

♥ Have you ever had a time when you were in need of comfort, and someone shared comfort they received from the Lord? How did that experience increase your connection with that person? With the Lord?

When God's comfort flows through His Spirit to His children and then flows between His children, God's family is connected, comforted, and looking more and more like their Father.

♥ Think about some of the affliction you've endured. Can you think of someone you know who may need some of the comfort you've received from the Lord?

♥ Think about some of the affliction you're enduring right now. (Maybe that lonely feeling!) Can you think of a Christian you know who has endured something similar? They may be able to comfort you with the comfort they've received from Christ! Consider reaching out to them today.

Today, you may feel deeply alone, but the truth is that God is with you more than you can fathom, and you are a part of a big, wonderful family.

♥ Take a moment to write a prayer asking the Holy Spirit to comfort you with God's truth and to connect you with your family.

Good News for When You Feel Ill-Equipped

"His divine power has given us everything required for life and godliness through the knowledge of him who called us by his own glory and goodness."
2 PETER 1:3

Sometimes I find this verse refreshing, and sometimes I give it side-eye because of the "everything" part. (Circle that word.) I'll think, "Really, God? You've given me everything I need for life and godliness?"

What helps the side-eye is paying closer attention. It's easy to lose interest in the second half starting with "through." (Underline that part in the verse above.) He's given us everything through our knowledge of Him. What does that mean? Let's investigate:

♥ Look up Exodus 3:11-12.

1. Based on verse 11, does Moses feel ill-equipped?

2. How does God respond?

Here we get a better look at what it means to have everything for life and godliness: God is with us.

Truth 1: God gives us Himself through His Spirit.

Moses didn't need training, a pep talk, or a bagel. God was with Him—Moses had all he needed! He just needed to know it.

♥ Interview yourself for a moment:

1. Do I know God is with me?

2. When and why do I doubt this?

3. How can I remind myself this is true?

Sister, if you are a Jesus follower, God's Spirit is not just with you but within you! It's the ultimate equipping. And yet, if we are not allowing the Holy Spirit to remind us what is true by reading God's Word and combating the lies that creep into our heads, we'll forget what we have. We will be like Moses, thinking about all that we lack rather than looking at Who is with us.

Truth 2: God gives us gifts through His Spirit.

God doesn't stop with His presence—He gives presents! (I had to.) Like the gift of comfort we talked about yesterday, these gifts are supposed to be re-gifted.

♥ Read the two passages below and make a list of all the gifts the Spirit gives in the chart below. (And keep a bookmark there, because we'll look back at both passages.)

1 Corinthians 12:4-11	1 Peter 4:10-11

These lists aren't comprehensive, but they are evidence the Spirit gives all kinds of gifts. He gives great gifts, but we want to be sure we keep our eye on the Giver.

Consider these two ideas:

♥ A gift is better when you know what you're supposed to use it for. Carefully read 1 Peter 4:10-11 again. For what two purposes does God want us to use His gifts?

1.

2.

♥ Some people obsess over determining what gift they have. But I think it's a better idea to walk by the Spirit.[2] Eventually, you'll look up and realize you are using your gift—it just seemed so natural, you didn't realize it was a gift! (God is good like that.) Have you ever seen that happen?

Even though God is with us and has given us gifts to use to serve, we know that having the Holy Spirit is not like getting bitten by a radioactive spider that gives us sudden spidey senses and the ability to shoot webs while wearing a red and blue unitard. Often there's that legitimate feeling: I don't have what I need.

This is true, too. (Am I confusing you yet?)

Truth 3: God gives us a family through His Spirit.

By design, you don't have everything as an individual—but God's family likely will! The Spirit gives different gifts to different people so we'll need one another.

♥ Can you think of a time when you were limited but someone else stepped in and offered what you needed?

But again, we can shift our gaze from the Giver to the gifts. Consider this:

♥ Look again at the 1 Corinthians passage from Truth #2. Though the gifts vary, what is the same for all believers?

♥ How could you use these passages to comfort and correct someone who feels jealous of the way God has gifted another person?

♥ So, has God given you everything you need?

Sister, good news: you have His Spirit, His Spirit's gift, and you have His family. You have everything you need for life and godliness—through the knowledge of Him! Don't forget what you know.

Good News for When Your "Want To" Is Broken

Though life is full of happy, sad, and angry moments, it's also full of "meh" moments—moments when, just, ugh, who cares? You know?

♥ Have you ever felt like that? Tell me about it.

I call myself "deeply and tragically lazy" for this reason. I get lots of stuff done, but there are moments when I cannot make myself care. The laundry is dirty? I cannot care. My hair is dirty? I cannot care. My soul is dirty? I cannot care.

♥ What do we do when our "want to" is broken?

There's a passage in Revelation that tends to thump me right in the middle of my lazy forehead. Revelation 3 ends with, "Let anyone who has ears to hear listen to what the Spirit says to the churches" (v. 22).

So what does the Spirit say to the churches? Plenty—but for today, let's just look at what the Spirit says to the church in Laodicea, a very wealthy city. Those who lived there probably had all they needed and wanted, and the result was a resounding: meh.

> [14] *"Write to the angel of the church in Laodicea: Thus says the Amen, the faithful and true witness, the originator of God's creation:* [15] *I know your works, that you are neither cold nor hot. I wish that you were cold or hot.* [16] *So, because you are lukewarm, and neither hot nor cold, I am going to vomit you out of my mouth.* [17] *For you say, 'I'm rich; I have become wealthy and need nothing,' and you don't realize that you are*

wretched, pitiful, poor, blind, and naked. [18] *I advise you to buy from me gold refined in the fire so that you may be rich, white clothes so that you may be dressed and your shameful nakedness not be exposed, and ointment to spread on your eyes so that you may see.* [19] *As many as I love, I rebuke and discipline. So be zealous and repent.* [20] *See! I stand at the door and knock. If anyone hears my voice and opens the door, I will come in to him and eat with him, and he with me."*

♥ Let's observe the text a bit more closely, trying to understand what it says:

1. Underline any descriptions that reveal their "meh" attitude.

2. What is the Spirit's response to their "meh" attitude?

3. Verse 17 shows us that though they may physically have everything, their spiritual condition is lacking. How does God describe it?

4. Based on this text, is spiritual "meh" (not caring about God or the things of God) dangerous? Is it sinful?

5. In verse 18, God advises them to buy three things from Him. Number those things in the text.

6. These are difficult words. According to verse 19, why is God speaking this way?

7. According to verse 20, does God want to be with these "meh" people?

8. What needs to happen for them to be together with God?

♥ Let's interpret the text a bit, trying to investigate what it means:

1. In verse 18, God advises them to buy from Him. Look up Isaiah 55:1. What is the cost for these things?

2. Think about the gospel truths you've learned so far in this study. What connections can you make with the list in verse 18?

♥ Finally, let's apply the text and remember the gospel, trying to discern how it should change the way we think and live:

1. Based on this text, if you are in a spiritually "meh" season, you may feel like you're fine. But how would you describe your true spiritual condition?

♥ Remember, sin is a devouring enemy—even when we can't feel its bite. Do you see any sin in your life that might have prompted your "meh" posture? Read Psalm 139:23-24 below, then write your answer.

> *Search me, God, and know my heart;*
> *test me and know my concerns.*
> *See if there is any offensive way in me;*
> *lead me in the everlasting way.*
> PSALM 139:23-24

♥ Remember what you've learned. Does God love you? Does He love you because someone makes Him or because He is truly, authentically loving?

♥ Is God like a grumpy, disappointed principal—or is He like a loving, tender father who delights in you, wants to provide for your needs, and welcomes you to His table?

When your "want to" is broken, bring every lazy bone to the Lord and ask God to help you die to yourself and live for Him.

♥ Use the space below to pray and invite the Holy Spirit to reveal your true spiritual condition, to remind you of your daughterhood, to remind you of the depth of His love and forgiveness.

_____

_____

_____

_____

_____

_____

_____

_____

_____

_____

Discovery

GOOD NEWS FOR WHEN YOU _____

- ♥ Take a few minutes and flip through this week's study pages. Considering all we've talked about this week, what is really sticking with you?

This week's big idea was the Holy Spirit—how He is our Helper in so many ways! (Remember the 7 Cs?)

- ♥ Take a deep breath, and then consider: Where do you need the help of the Holy Spirit?

- ♥ Based on all we've learned about the Holy Spirit, what good news can you offer yourself for that place of struggle in your life? (If you can't think of something personal right now, perhaps you have a friend who is struggling in one of these areas. What good news can you offer her?)

Let's close with two gospel verses. Read them over carefully so you don't overlook their good news:

"There is salvation in no one else, for there is no other name under heaven given to people by which we must be saved."
Acts 4:12

He escorted them out and said, "Sirs, what must I do to be saved?" They said, "Believe in the Lord Jesus, and you will be saved—you and your household."
Acts 16:30-31

We spend most of our time in this study talking about how the gospel is good news for our **everyday specifics.** But the gospel is also good news for our **eternal salvation.** Only God can truly save us! Remember, anyone who calls upon the name of the Lord will be saved—from their sins, from death, to a family, forever. When we believe in our hearts that Jesus died for our sins, lives again, and that because of this, God will forgive us, we are saved! We are no longer His sin-soaked enemies but forgiven and fathered forever.

Is this something you sense the Holy Spirit is stirring in you to do? Do you desire to put yourself under God's loving leadership forever? If so, ask Him to save you! Then, tell someone who loves Jesus: "I am a Christian now!" so they can celebrate with you.

P.S. Some people feel the nudge to "get saved" a lot. But once you are God's child, you are His child forever! You don't have to keep joining the family. If you are confused about this, ask a trusted Christian leader to help you discern it. You may consider reading 1 John or John 10:27-29 together.

Jesus's Return

SESSION 7

Group time

THIS STUDY IS ALL ABOUT GOOD NEWS!

What's some good news you got this week?

What's some bad news you got this week?

Is there any good news hidden inside the bad news?

What good news can you remember from last week's group session and study days?

INTRODUCTION

♥ Can you believe we are at the final part of the gospel definition? There are seven parts of the definition. See if you can remember each part:

1.

2.

3.

4.

5.

6.

7.

♥ Is there are particular aspect of the gospel that has had special meaning for you lately? If you can, share about that with your group.

Jesus is the middle part of our definition, but He's also the beginning and the end! This week, we're talking about the glorious end of the story—when Jesus comes back. But first, let's look back to see Jesus at the beginning.

♥ Look up John 1:1. How does this verse enhance our understanding of who Jesus is?

WATCH

As you watch the Session 7 video with your group, fill in the blanks below.

Every _____ of our hearts is a neon arrow pointing to something_____ — the _____ coming.

When _____ returns, He will make all things _____ and _____ forever.

Make a list of good things Revelation 21–22 tells us are coming for God's children when Jesus returns. (Hint: Most of the good news is either something that's (1) made NEW or (2) something that's NO MORE.)

We can look to Jesus's _____ and know that one day, every _____ thing will be made _____.

EXAMINATION

Let's take a moment to examine one particular angle of Jesus's return: our bodies.

♥   Look up 1 Thessalonians 4:16-18. What will happen to our bodies when Jesus comes back?

When Jesus was resurrected, His body was made new. When He comes back, our bodies will be resurrected too—made new, like Him! This helps us understand that our bodies matter. They aren't throwaway things.

♥   Do you ever treat your body like it doesn't matter? Tell me about it.

On the other hand, Jesus's return helps us understand that we don't have to feel the burden to make our bodies new. That's His job!

♥   Do you ever long for your body to be made new? Why?

While we wait for Jesus to return, how might the reality of the resurrection impact the way we view and use our bodies?

♥   Look up Revelation 22:20. When does Jesus say He's coming?

When Jesus says He's coming "soon" or "quickly" that can feel really confusing to us. Because it can seem like He's, well, taking His time. But this word is probably vague by design.

♥ Look up Matthew 24:36-38. Who knows when Jesus is coming back? Who doesn't know?

It's important to remember something we learned at the very beginning: Yahweh has no limits of time, space, and knowledge. The way our human minds understand "soon" may be a little different than He understands it.

♥ Look up 2 Peter 3:9 and write it below:

♥ Based on this verse, why has Jesus not yet returned?

If Yahweh has no limits of time, space, and knowledge, and if Yahweh is good, we can trust that He will return at the perfect time. A.T. Pierson once described Christ's return by saying it's "certain to occur at some time, uncertain at what time."[1]

As we wait on the uncertain time, we can wait with certainty by recounting what God has promised. This is why it's so wonderful that we have chapters in the Bible like Revelation 21–22 that we can look to when things feel shaky and hopeless!

In the teaching video, we looked over these chapters and made a list of so many of the wonderful things that will happen when Jesus returns. Look back over them and see if there's anything we missed. Then, take some time to ponder the list with your group.

💜 Is there anything in the text that confuses you? Talk it out based on what you know about God and His gospel.

💜 What thrills you the most? Why?

APPLICATION

Every longing of our hearts is a neon arrow to something better: the second advent when Christ comes again. I imagine it's like being a character in a Cinderella story, living in a cold attic and interacting with people who don't know how to truly love you. You hear your true father is coming home to rescue you and take you to a home that is safer, sweeter, and more wonderful than anything you could possibly imagine.

Oh, how we long for our God and our true home and our forever family that no one can break! Oh, how we long for our pain, tears, and grief to melt away in the light of His glory!

💜 Revelation 22:20 is the cry of every Christian's heart. Write it below.

PRAY

Christians throughout history have prayed these words in faith, knowing He will come. They are also praying with longing, knowing Jesus's return will dull their pain and catapult their worship into full color.

💜 Is there a particular area of your life that makes your heart cry out, "Come, Lord Jesus!"? If so, consider sharing it with you group. Then, take time to pray together, "Come, Lord Jesus!"

♥ Then, read this out loud together. (I know this might be awkward, but go with it!)

> **Group Leader**: When Jesus returns, we will be truly together with Him in a way our souls have always longed to be.

> **Students**: We will be truly together with one another in a forever family no one can break.

> **Everyone**: We will be truly whole and healed, because pain no longer exists, tears no longer fall, death no longer happens, and our great enemy sin no longer threatens us.

> **Group Leader**: Are you longing for that?

> **Students**: We are.

> **Group Leader**: And so you should be. Longing for something is exactly right and good—so long as you keep your eyes up.

> **Everyone**: Take comfort, sisters, and have courage: Our King is coming.

Close your prayer time by praising God for the good news of the gospel and asking Him to help you and your group to grasp it in a deeper way.

Good News for When You Feel Like It Will Never Get Better

There's good news for when you feel like it will never get better. Not only will it indeed get "better," but "better" is an understatement.

♥ Read Revelation 21:1-8 below. As you read, draw an "up arrow" above anything that's been made better.

> [1] Then I saw a new heaven and a new earth; for the first heaven and the first earth had passed away, and the sea was no more. [2] I also saw the holy city, the new Jerusalem, coming down out of heaven from God, prepared like a bride adorned for her husband. [3] Then I heard a loud voice from the throne: Look, God's dwelling is with humanity, and he will live with them. They will be his peoples, and God himself will be with them and will be their God. [4] He will wipe away every tear from their eyes. Death will be no more; grief, crying, and pain will be no more, because the previous things have passed away. [5] Then the one seated on the throne said, "Look, I am making everything new." He also said, "Write, because these words are faithful and true." [6] Then he said to me, "It is done! I am the Alpha and the Omega, the beginning and the end. I will freely give to the thirsty from the spring of the water of life. [7] The one who conquers will inherit these things, and I will be his God, and he will be my son. [8] But the cowards, faithless, detestable, murderers, sexually immoral, sorcerers, idolaters, and all liars—their share will be in the lake that burns with fire and sulfur, which is the second death."

♥ Let's observe the text a bit more closely, trying to discern what it says by answering the following questions:

1. The passage starts with a wedding image. Who is the bride? How is she dressed?

2. Think about what you know about brides and how they "adorn themselves." How does that help you understand verse 2?

3. Verse 3 contains an announcement. Where does God live now?

4. God has always been with His people, but what clues do you have that this "with" will be better?

5. In *The Lord of the Rings* trilogy, Sam Gamgee says to Gandalf, "Is everything sad going to come untrue?"[2] In verse 4, number the list of things that will go away.

6. A big theme in this passage is newness. Circle the word "new" wherever you see it.

7. According to verse 6, what does God give? To whom does He give it? How does He give it?

8. Two opposite groups are mentioned in verses 7 and 8. Describe the two groups.

The New Jerusalem is the bride in this passage. In the Old Testament, we see that Jerusalem represents God's people. New Testament writers say that the church (everyone who follows God) is the bride of Christ. Whether we say Jerusalem, God's followers, or the church, all of these terms refer to the same thing: believers! We are part of the Bride of Christ, and on the day Jesus returns for us, we will be as radiant as a bride, and Jesus will look at us with all the joy and affection of a loving groom.

1. Verse 7 tells us that all of these better things in the passage are inherited by "the one who conquers." Look up verse Revelation 12:11 and fill in the blank: "They conquered him [Satan] by_____."

2. Everything is lovely until verse 8, and then we swerve into unquotable territory. What do you know about the gospel that can help you process this? (Go back to page 120 for help to answer this.)

3. What is the difference between the group that conquers and the group that is punished?

4. How is it good news that God, even in the new heaven and new earth, still treats sin like a big deal?

Sister, life is long, and it really can feel as if things will never get better. But this is why we look ahead to what God has promised. One day, He will make all things new, and all terrible things will melt away. Those who are covered by the blood of the Lamb will be with God in a new and better way. How safe and wonderful this place will be!

♥ List three things from today's reading that give you hope that it really will get better, and ask the Holy Spirit to call them to mind when you struggle with hopelessness.

PERSONAL STUDY 2

Good News for When Nothing Satisfies

It's the classic December 26th condition: Christmas is over, and it didn't quite satisfy. This frustrating scenario (that can also happen post-vacation, after birthdays, etc.), is "old earth" stuff. Until Jesus returns, dissatisfaction gnaws at us. We combat this with gratitude for what God has given now and hope for what He will give.

Let's pick up where we left off in Revelation 21. The passage continues in verse 9 with an angel saying, "Come, I will show you the bride, the wife of the Lamb."

That beautiful bride was the new city of Jerusalem—which represents all of God's people—and now we get to see what she looks like. Just like weddings you've attended or see in movies, abundance is a big theme. Abundance has two meanings: lots of stuff and luxurious stuff.[3]

♥ Read Revelation 21:10–22:5 in your Bible and keep an eye out for anything delightfully abundant.

♥ Let's observe this passage, and to better understand what it says, answer the following questions:

1. How does verse 11 describe the appearance of the bride?

2. What number is repeated in verses 12-14? This number corresponds with two groups. What are the two groups? (Hint: Group 1 is mentioned in verse 12 and Group 2 is mentioned in verse 14.)

3. Verses 15-17 describe the measurements of the city. These measurements mirror the Most Holy Place in the temple, where God's presence dwelled. (Whoa!) Then, verses 18-21 describe the building materials of the city. Which of the features fascinates you the most?

4. In "old earth," Jerusalem's main feature was always the temple because God dwelt there. Why, in new Jerusalem, is there no temple (v. 22)?

5. Why is there no need for the sun, moon, or lamps (v. 23)?

6. People from all over the world who follow Jesus will come into this city (vv. 24-26)! But according to verse 27, what is not allowed in?

7. "Water of life" is a theme we see throughout Scripture. How is it described in Revelation 22:1? How does this track with that theme of abundance?

8. The tree of life is mentioned in verse 2. How is it described?

As we continue in Revelation 22:3-5, we see the earth is no longer cursed by sin, God's children are fully His in every way, wearing His name on their foreheads, there is no night, and God's heirs will reign with Him forever. Wow!

❤ Let's interpret a few things in this passage that may need some uncovering:

1. In Revelation 21:12-14, we noticed two groups of twelve: The tribes of Israel and the apostles. The tribes of Israel grew because Israel's twelve sons had children, and their children had children, and so on. Look up Matthew 28:19. How did the twelve apostles grow?

2.   Notably, then in Revelation 21:24-26, we see the nations coming to God's city. Look up Isaiah 60:3-5. How does this seem like the most epic family reunion?

3.   In Genesis 3, the tree of life just has one fruit. Read Revelation 22:2-3. How is the tree of life different now?

4.   What happened to the curse that was given after Adam and Eve ate from that other, forbidden tree?

5.   Think about the people and the trees. How is the new heaven and new earth a picture of abundance and satisfaction?

Revelation 21–22 remind us that God is a God of abundance and satisfaction. But do you ever think of Him as withholding things from you? Do you ever feel tempted to look for satisfaction outside of Him and what He's provided?

♥   How does today's reading remind you that true satisfaction awaits?

♥   How can you remind yourself of this truth when you struggle to want full satisfaction now?

♥   In some ways, why is our "old earth" dissatisfaction a good thing? In other words, what are those "hunger pangs" ultimately pointing us to?

Good News for When You Are Burnt Out and Want to Give Up

Have you ever said in frustration, "I'm over this"? It's a common feeling—wanting to toss our hands up and quit. It makes sense because, well, life is really hard sometimes. And yet we see throughout Scripture the call to endure, to be faithful, to keep going even when we feel we can't. Christians know we are able to endure by God's power alone—we are too weak! But why should we stay faithful? And how are we supposed to do it?

Faithful means "steadfast in affection or allegiance."[4] In other words, a faithful person is one who keeps loving and stays loyal to whomever they promised their love and loyalty. Hebrews 11 is called the Faith Chapter because it lists people throughout the Old Testament who followed God despite great adversity. The list contains some scrappy individuals, leading the reader to discover that these people were only faithful because God was so very faithful.

The people in Hebrews 11 didn't live perfectly faithful lives—they simply believed God was faithful to them. (In the Christian faith, it's always God's faithfulness that is at the center of the story!) That belief was credited to them as righteousness. Then, there was overflow: Their faith gushed out into how they lived.

Hebrews 12 begins by referencing this "faith list," and then helps us understand the how and why of our faith journeys:

1. **How** we can live a faithful life.

2. **Why** we should live a faithful life.

HOW

> [1] *Therefore, since we also have such a large cloud of witnesses surrounding us, let us lay aside every hindrance and the sin that so easily ensnares us. Let us run with endurance the race that lies before us,* [2] *keeping our eyes on Jesus, the pioneer and perfecter of our faith. For the joy that lay before him, he endured the cross, despising the shame, and sat down at the right hand of the throne of God.*
> HEBREWS 12:1-2

♥ Let's observe this passage to better understand what it says:

1. To run with endurance, what do we need to lay aside?

2. Where do we need to keep our eyes?

3. Why did Jesus endure the cross?

4. What did Jesus do after He endured the cross?

♥ Let's apply the text to our lives:

1. According to the writer of Hebrews, how can you as a Christian live a faithful life, even when things are hard?

2. When you are burned out and want to give up, you can ask yourself two things (go ahead and answer them now, too!):

   a. What do I need to lay aside?

   b. Where are my eyes?

The gospel is good news for the girl who needs to lay aside sin—because God Himself conquered sin! The gospel is good news for the girl whose eyes are on herself or on the world—because Jesus offers the hope and rest she longs for!

WHY

We also want to consider why we endure as Christians. What's our motivation?

♥ Read Hebrews 12:1-2 again.

This passage talks about (1) the fact that Jesus endured the cross and (2) the fact that He is ruling in a royal place of honor right now.

♥ Knowing these two things, why should we endure? In other words, how can these two gospel truths motivate us to stay faithful?

♥ Open your Bible to the spot we left off yesterday. Read Revelation 22:6-21. (The very last words of the whole Bible!)

♥ Make a list of anything that might encourage a weary traveler to keep going. Especially keep an eye out for the word "come," which is repeated quite a bit.

Sister, when we are soul-thirsty and weary from journeying, we can keep our eyes on Jesus, and we can remember that His return offers two beautiful pieces of good news in these Scripture passages:

> *"Let the one who is thirsty come. Let the one who desires take the water of life freely."*
> REVELATION 22:17

> *"I am coming soon"*
> REVELATION 22:12,20

Amen! Come, Lord Jesus!

Discovery Page

GOOD NEWS FOR WHEN YOU_____

- ♥ Take a few minutes and flip through this week's study pages. Considering all we've talked about this week, what is really sticking with you?

- ♥ This week's big idea was Jesus's return! Was there anything that surprised you? Tell me about it!

- ♥ Take a moment to pause and consider how that big idea intersects with your current struggles.

When we are longing for something, waiting for something, discontent or frustrated with the way things are, Jesus's return is really good news.

- ♥ Let's get specific with where you are right now: Where are you hungry for things to be made right? What are you longing for?

- ♥ Based on all we've learned about Jesus's return, what good news can you offer yourself for that place of struggle in your life? (If you can't think of something personal right now, perhaps you have a friend who is struggling in one of these areas. What good news can you offer her?)

Let's close with two gospel verses. Read them over carefully so you don't overlook their good news:

For all have sinned and fall short of the glory of God; they are justified freely by his grace through the redemption that is in Christ Jesus.
ROMANS 3:23-24

"See! I stand at the door and knock. If anyone hears my voice and opens the door, I will come in to him and eat with him, and he with me."
REVELATION 3:20

We spend most of our time in this study talking about how the gospel is good news for our **everyday specifics.** But the gospel is also good news for our **eternal salvation.** The gospel is an invitation—like Romans 3:20 describes as a knock at the door. When we hear the knock, we get the glorious honor of opening the door. This means welcoming God into every part of us and submitting to the truths He proclaims, like "all have sinned." We agree with Him that we are sinners deserving death, yet we believe that Jesus endured death instead and shares His new life with those who follow Him. When we "answer the door," we are confessing our sin and submitting ourselves to God's loving leadership forever. Then we are no longer His sin-soaked enemies but forgiven and fathered forever!

Is this something you sense the Holy Spirit is stirring in you to do? If so, ask Him to save you! Then, tell someone who loves Jesus: "I am a Christian now!" so they can celebrate with you.

P.S. Some people feel the nudge to "get saved" a lot. But once you are God's child, you are His child forever! You don't have to keep joining the family. If you are confused about this, ask a trusted Christian leader to help you discern it. You may consider reading 1 John or John 10:27-29 together.

SEE THE GOSPEL + SING THE GOSPEL

SESSION 8

Group time

THIS STUDY IS ALL ABOUT GOOD NEWS!

What's some good news you got this week?

What's some bad news you got this week?

Is there any good news hidden inside the bad news?

What good news can you remember from last week's group session and study days?

INTRODUCTION

♥ Do you know the gospel definition? Try to say it out loud with all seven parts.

♥ List the seven parts below, and try to explain why each part is good news for you.

1.

2.

3.

4.

5.

6.

7.

♥ Which part surprised you the most?

♥ Has there been a part that you've noticed yourself thinking about often? Which part? Why do you think it keeps coming to mind?

We spent most of our time in this study talking about how the gospel is good news for our everyday specifics. But the gospel is also good news for our eternal salvation.

♥ Look up Revelation 3:20 and Romans 10:9. Have you ever sensed Jesus "knocking on the door"? Have you responded like Romans 10:9 says?

♥ Read 2 Corinthians 1:4. What kind of gospel comfort have you received in your life that you might be able to offer to others?

WATCH

As you watch the Session 8 video with your group, fill in the blanks below.

The gospel is not just good news for _____—it's good news for _____ you know.

What God _____ over you, you can _____ over others.

_____ the gospel and let it go to _____ in your everyday life!

You can read my "Mirror Mantra" on page 140.

The good news won't _____ the pain and reality of the bad news—but it helps address it and _____ our gaze to the One who will make all things _____ one day.

We tell the gospel not like ones who _____ it all, but like ones who have been _____ of it all.

BE GOSPEL SINGERS

This week is all about being filled up with the gospel and splashing it out onto other people. It's my prayer that you will be a spectacularly messy Christian, sloshing gospel goodness everywhere! I want it to rise up in you and spill out of you until you and your family and friends are utterly drenched, soaked to the soul.

Because of this, I want you and your group to spend your time together compassionately and carefully seeking to notice where your loved ones are struggling and how the gospel is good news for them. Let's do this with (1) sensitivity, not oversharing stories that aren't ours to share, and (2) humility, knowing that there's only one Savior—Jesus. We can't save! We can just point to the One who saves. With that in mind, consider the following questions together:

♥ Take a few minutes for yourself and think of your family and friends. What "pain points" do you notice? What are their struggles?

Without mentioning names or super-specific details, have each group member share something from their list. As a group, try to discern how the gospel is good news for that particular person and pain point. It's okay if this takes up most of your time together!

When you know the gospel is good news for someone in a specific way, that doesn't mean you need to go beat down your friend's door and say, "HERE'S THE GOSPEL!" and shove it in their face like you're force-feeding them cake. Instead, ask the Holy Spirit to help you know when to speak.

♥ Read Psalm 139:4 together.

Psalm 139:4 can help us trust the Holy Spirit when He nudges, "Shhh! Not now!" or when He says, "It's time to speak." Why? Because Yahweh doesn't just know your words—He knows the mind and heart of the person who will hear your words.

♥ Look up Psalm 139:1-2 and write the verses below.

♥ Spend some time praying that the Holy Spirit will help each girl know when to speak good news to those who need to hear it.

Sister, the gospel is good news for you when you are afraid to share the gospel. When you fail to obey, you are covered by Christ's righteousness. When you stutter over your words, you are deeply loved. When you feel afraid you'll look stupid, the Holy Spirit is within you, reminding you that you aren't alone. When you are faithful to obey, the Holy Spirit is at work in you, making you more like Jesus.

The gospel is always good news, and I hope you'll be a gospel singer, singing the truth over those who long for it in a tone that honors the beauty of the message.

♥ Have you ever heard the right thing said in the wrong way? How did the tone change what you heard?

♥ As a group, consider what it looks like to share the gospel in a way that honors the beauty of the message.

Gospel singers, here's a good place to start:

♥ How specifically is the gospel good news for you today? Well, go tell someone that. Who can you tell?

♥ Why is it important to sing the gospel over yourself, too?

♥ When is a time you're especially prone to forget the gospel?

♥ How can you remind one another of the gospel?

There's always good news, sisters, if you will make sure you look for it! Please keep seeing it as if you have gospel glasses planted on your face. Please keep singing it with a tone as lovely as the message.

May the gospel take root in your heart and grow and grow, till it grows out your ears, till it makes good news out of everything you see. And as you sing the good news to a world desperate for its melody:

> "May the LORD bless you and protect you;
> may the LORD make his face shine on you
> and be gracious to you;
> may the LORD look with favor on you
> and give you peace."
> NUMBERS 6:24-26

LEADER GUIDE

Leader tips

PRAY DILIGENTLY.

Ask God to prepare you to lead this study. Pray individually and specifically for the girls in your group. Make this a priority in your personal walk and preparation.

PREPARE ADEQUATELY.

Don't just wing this. Take time to preview each session so you have a good grasp of the content. Look over the group session and consider your girls. Feel free to delete, reword, or add questions that fit your group better.

Please note: There is an important disclaimer to read on Personal Study Day 1 of Session 1. Talk with your church leaders if you have any further questions or concerns about this content matter.

PROVIDE RESOURCES.

Each girl will need a Bible study book. Try to have extras on hand for those who join the group later in the study. Also suggest girls bring a Bible and journal to group each week.

ENCOURAGE FREELY.

Cheer for your girls and encourage them to participate in every part of the study.

LEAD BY EXAMPLE.

Make sure you complete all of the personal study. Be willing to share your story, what you're learning, and your own questions with the group.

BE AWARE.

If girls are hesitant to discuss their thoughts and questions in a large group, consider a small group setting more conducive to conversation.

FOLLOW UP.

If a girl mentions a prayer request or need, make sure to follow up. It may be a situation where the group can get involved in helping out.

EVALUATE OFTEN.

After each session, assess what needs to be changed to more effectively lead the study.

Looking for social assets to share with your girls or their parents?

SCAN THIS QR CODE

Let's talk about Group time

GETTING STARTED

Each group time starts with a chance for your girls to share good and bad news from their week. Help make it interactive and be willing to share your high and low points, too. Be mindful that this is just the start of your time together and keep the conversation flowing quickly. If you have a large group, have the girls pair up to share their answers rather than discussing with the whole group.

INTRODUCTION

This section is to help your girls reflect on what they've been learning in order to launch into the new session. Be ready to break down the different elements of the gospel every week and challenge the girls to memorize the full gospel definition found on page 8.

WATCH

To help build the foundation for your group discussion, you will want to watch each of the teaching videos. These videos are available to buy or rent as a separate purchase at lifeway.com/goodnews. Each video will last approximately 12-17 minutes. Encourage your girls to follow along by taking notes and filling in the blanks. See the answers below:

- Session 1: Elohim; humans, demand, with; LORD, Yahweh; Limitless, Unchanging, Present, Self-existent; Character

- Session 2: Sin, Sin; boundary, living, live; enemy, enemy; Sin, okay, sin; God, sin; God, sin, against; good, news, sees, enemy, ignore

- Session 3: life, death, new life; message, means, Himself; life, gospel, imputation; righteous, Christ, righteousness; status, status, steps

- Session 4: death, rescue; clothing, curse; sin, punishes, forgiven; sin, shame; all, covered

- Session 5: Jesus, deserved, life; resurrection, love; mercy, covering; death, death; power, circumstances; meet, God

- Session 6: Himself, Father, Son, Holy Spirit; love, work; followers, you, you; creations, automatically

- Session 7: longing, better, second; Jesus, new, wonderful; return, terrible, beautiful

- Session 8: you, everyone; sings, sings; learn, work; dismiss, points, new; know, forgiven

EXAMINATION

It's time to jump into the discussion! Walk your girls through the different questions and Scripture passages provided in this section. It will always help to come prepared ahead of time in order to anticipate what your group might want to focus their time on in this section.

APPLICATION

Now it's time for girls to actually apply what you've been talking about. There will be questions to help prompt both discussion and reflection. Use discretion on how you want to handle this time based on the maturity of your group. It might benefit the girls to work in smaller groups, especially if you have additional leaders.

Please note: There is a journaling section in Session 4 that asks girls to get real with God. This might be a great opportunity to allow girls to spread out around the room with some music playing to help create a safe space.

PRAY

You don't want to skip this time in your group! Also, sessions 7 and 8 will look different than the first six sessions, so make sure to plan accordingly.

MIRROR MANTRA

God made this body, this hair, this skin, and He gave them to me. Thank you, God!

Because sin is at work inside and outside this body, God came to live in a body, like me.

Because God loves me, God gave His body for me. Thank you, God!

Because God loves me, I will use my body to bring Him glory. He will help me.

Because God loves me, I will love this body He gave me. He will help me.

Thank you, God!

 Want your own copy to make your phone screensaver or to print and hang in your bathroom? Check out this QR code to find a version you can download!

End Notes

Session 1

1. Milton Vincent, *A Gospel Primer for Christians* (Focus Publishing, 2008) 31.
2. For more insight into what Yahweh means, visit "10 Things Yahweh Means," John Piper, *Desiring God*, August 5, 2022, https://www.desiringgod.org/articles/10-things-yahweh-means.
3. Strong's H3519, *Blue Letter Bible*, https://www.blueletterbible.org/lexicon/h3519/kjv/wlc/0-1/.
4. Jeremy Bouma, "Psalm 121 Commentary: Where Does Our Help Come From?" *Zondervan Academic*, October 12, 2018, https://zondervanacademic.com/blog/psalm-121-commentary-where-does-our-help-come-from.

Session 2

1. Martin Lloyd-Jones, *Seeking the Face of God: Nine Reflections on the Psalms* (Wheaton, IL: Crossway, 2005), 34.

Session 3

1. *Merriam-Webster*, s.v. "incarnate," https://www.merriam-webster.com/dictionary/incarnate.

Session 4

1. "Christ Alone" by Matthew Barrett from *Sola: How the Five Solas Are Still Reforming the Church* by Jason K. Allen, General Editor (Chicago: Moody Publishers, 2019) 89.
2. *Merriam-Webster*, s.v. "refuge," https://www.merriam-webster.com/dictionary/refuge.

Session 5

1. Strong's H3727, *Blue Letter Bible*, https://www.blueletterbible.org/lexicon/h3727/kjv/wlc/0-1/.
2. Ligon Duncan, "Propitiation," *The Gospel Coalition*, https://www.thegospelcoalition.org/essay/propitiation/.
3. Strong's H3727.
4. C.S. Lewis, *The Lion, the Witch, and the Wardrobe* (New York: Harper, 1950) 178-179.
5. David Guzik, "John 11," *Enduring God*, https://enduringword.com/bible-commentary/john-11/.
6. C.S. Lewis, *The Magician's Nephew* (New York: Harper, 1950) 168.

Session 6

1. *Merriam-Webster*, s.v. "affliction," https://www.merriam-webster.com/dictionary/affliction.
2. Thomas Schreiner, "How (Not) to Discover Your Spiritual Gifts," *The Gospel Coalition*, July 6, 2018, https://www.thegospelcoalition.org/article/how-not-discover-spiritual-gifts/.

Session 7

1. *Prophetic Studies of the International Prophetic Conference: Chicago, November 1886* (Chicago: F.H. Revel, 1886) 27.
2. J.R.R. Tolkien, *The Return of the King* (New York: HarperCollins, 1966) 215.
3. *Merriam-Webster*, s.v. "abundance," https://www.merriam-webster.com/dictionary/abundance.
4. *Merriam-Webster*, s.v. "faithful," https://www.merriam-webster.com/dictionary/faithful.

Notes

Notes

Get the most from your study.

Customize your Bible study time with a guided experience and additional resources.

ADDITIONAL
RESOURCES

GOOD NEWS EBOOK
An eight-session study on how to know the gospel and live it.

GOOD NEWS VIDEO STREAMING BUNDLE
Hear from author, Caroline Saunders, in these eight teaching videos.

Heard any good news lately?

Some days we feel like we're on top of the world. We ace the test, make the team, and get the guy! But other days it feels like the world is spinning out of control. We don't quite measure up, we fail big-time, and no one even seems to notice we exist. So, where's the good news on those days?

In this new eight-session study by *Better Than Life* author Caroline Saunders, girls will learn how to discover the good news of the gospel in every circumstance and in all aspects of their lives. They'll learn not only the doctrine of salvation, but the experience of salvation. The good news Jesus brings isn't just "future" good news; it's good news for today, too.

Want to watch the *Good News* teaching videos when and where it is most convenient? Introducing the Lifeway On Demand app! From your smartphone to your TV, watching videos from Lifeway has never been easier.

Available in the **Lifeway On Demand** app

Stream on these devices:
ROKU **tv** **fire** tv

App Store Google Play

For more information about Lifeway Girls, visit lifeway.com/girls.